ASSESSMENT IN COLLEGE LIBRARY INSTRUCTION PROGRAMS

CLIP Note #32

Compiled by

Lawrie H. Merz
Beth L. Mark
Messiah College
Grantham, Pennsylvania

College Library Information Packet Committee
College Libraries Section
Association of College and Research Libraries
A Division of the American Library Association
Chicago 2002

The paper used in this publication meets the minimum requirements of American National Standard for Information Sciences–Permanence of Paper for Printed Library Materials, ANSI Z39.48-1992. ∞

Library of Congress Cataloging-in-Publication Data

Merz, Lawrie H.
  Assessment in college library instruction programs/Lawrie H. Merz and Beth L. Mark.
    p. cm.-- (CLIP note ; #32)
Includes bibliographical references.
  ISBN 0-8389-8201-8 (alk. paper)
  1. Library orientation for college students--United
States--Evaluation. 2. Information literacy--Study and teaching
(Higher)--United States. 3. Information literacy--Ability
testing--United States. 4. Library surveys--United States. I. Mark,
Beth L. II. Association of College and Research Libraries. College
Library Information Packet Committee. III. Title. IV. CLIP notes ; #32.
  Z711.2 .M47 2002
  025.5'677'0973--dc21

                                                        2002007308

Printed on recycled paper.

Printed in the United States of America.

06 05 04 03 02   5 4 3 2 1

TABLE OF CONTENTS

University of Charleston
Schoenbaum Library
Charleston, West Virginia

Houghton College *(final project)*
Willard J. Houghton Library
Houghton, New York

Lynchburg College *(test on electronic research)*
Knight-Capron Library
Lynchburg, Virginia

Manhattanville College *(final project)*
Manhattanville College Library
Purchase, New York

Messiah College *(general test)*
Murray Library
Grantham, Pennsylvania

San Francisco State University *(sample quiz questions)*
J. Paul Leonard Library
San Francisco, California

Shepherd College *(general test)*
Ruth Scarborough Library
Shepherdstown, West Virginia

University of North Carolina at Asheville *(sample exam questions)*
D. Hiden Ramsey Library
Asheville, North Carolina

University of Southern Colorado *(general test)*
University of Southern Colorado Library
Pueblo, Colorado

West Texas A & M University *(take-home exam)*
Cornette Library
Canyon, Texas

Georgia Southwestern State University
James Earl Carter Library
Americus, Georgia

Houghton College
Willard J. Houghton Library
Houghton, New York

Lander University
Jackson Library
Greenwood, South Carolina

Lynchburg College
Knight-Capron Library
Lynchburg, Virginia

University of St. Thomas
O'Shaughnessy-Frey Library
St. Paul, Minnesota

University of Southern Colorado
University of Southern Colorado Library
Pueblo, Colorado

Whitworth College
Harriet Cheney Cowles Memorial Library
Spokane, Washington

Eastern Washington University
John F. Kennedy Library
Cheney, Washington

Emerson College
Emerson College Library
Boston, Massachusetts

Gettysburg College
Musselman Library
Gettysburg, Pennsylvania

Lynchburg College
Knight-Capron Library
Lynchburg, Virginia

Ursuline College
Ralph M. Besse Library
Pepper Pike, Ohio

CLIP NOTES COMMITTEE

Jody Caldwell, Chair
Drew University Library
Drew University
Madison, New Jersey

Rhonna A.Goodman
Manhattanville College Library
Manhattanville College
Purchase, New York

David P. Jensen
Van Wylen Library
Hope College
Holland, Michigan

Christopher B. Loring
William Allan Neilson Library
Smith College
Northampton, Massachusetts

Nancy Newins
McGraw-Page Library
Randolph-Macon College
Ashland, Virginia

Jennifer Phillips
James Branch Cabell Library
Virginia Commonwealth University
Richmond, Virginia

Brian Rossmann
Montana State University Libraries
Montana State University
Bozeman, Montana

Gene Ruffin
Gwinnett University Center
Gwinnett Technical College
Lawrenceville, Georgia

Marcia L. Thomas
Ames Library
Illinois Wesleyan University
Bloomington, Illinois

Ann Watson
Doane Library
Denison University
Granville, Ohio

Corey Williams Green
Russell D. Cole Library
Cornell College
Mt. Vernon, Iowa

David Wright
Leland Speed Library
Mississippi College
Clinton, Mississippi

Thanks to three students from Messiah College's Business Information Systems
program--Jason Long, Andy Binkiwitz, and Dave Lanzer--who assisted with the data analysis as
part of a class project. And special thanks to Emily Hayes,
our tireless workstudy student, whose help proved invaluable.

INTRODUCTION

BACKGROUND

College-level library instruction in the United States has been evolving since the late 1800s. It was not until the 1960s, however, that a sustained interest in library instruction developed from the grassroots and began to have an impact on the library field (Seamans, 2001). A shift in focus from providing library orientation/tours for students to librarians teaching library or bibliographic instruction did not occur until the early 1970s (Rader, 1993). At that time librarians began educating themselves about classroom techniques, learning styles, and more, while initiating discussions with faculty to incorporate course-related library instruction into their classes. A pivotal change in thinking about the field of library instruction and its nomenclature occurred in 1985 when a working definition for "information literacy" was developed by Martin Tessmer: "Information literacy is the ability to effectively access and evaluate information for a given need" (Breivik, 1985). In 1989, an expansion of this definition, with which librarians are familiar today, was developed by the American Library Association's Presidential Committee on Information Literacy whose final report was widely disseminated (1989). Higher education's acceptance of the definition led into the decade of the 1990s when librarians spent significant time analyzing the concept of information literacy and tried to determine how it related to current and future programs on their campuses. The next logical step was to clearly articulate what student learning outcomes were expected and then how to develop ways of assessing the outcomes.

Little was written about assessing student outcomes in the area of information literacy until the 1990s. Well-attended conference workshops on assessment were offered at an increasing rate and reflect the high interest in assessment both then and now. Unfortunately, for the majority of colleges and universities, high interest has not resulted in large numbers of well-designed assessment tools. There are understandable obstacles: lack of systematic and/or longitudinal access to students due to reliance on the good graces of classroom faculty (Rabine, 2000); inadequate staffing; little or no access to appropriate teaching facilities; or lack of institutional support.

Librarians are motivated to implement effective assessment programs for at least two reasons: external pressure imposed by accrediting agencies that require "evidence" of student learning and a desire to improve student learning through improved teaching methods that are informed by assessment findings (Rabine, 2000).

A meaningful assessment program must start by identifying and documenting the desired student learning outcomes (Iannuzzi, 1999). With the recent adoption of ACRL's *Information Literacy Competency Standards for Higher Education* (2000), the profession has been provided with a benchmark for assessment. After outcomes are established, the type of assessment needs to be selected. Two standard categories of assessment in higher education are **formative**, which measures the quality of instruction, and **summative**, which measures actual learning (Riddle & Hartman, 2000). Examples of formative assessments are surveys and other self-assessed student learning such as the one-minute paper, and identification of either what was learned or what the muddiest (most confusing) point was. Summative assessment is comprised of assessment methods such as tests, portfolios, bibliography analysis, and analyses of term papers (Stewart, 1999).

Librarians can learn from each other by studying how other libraries are doing assessment. This *CLIP Note* provides several good examples of information literacy assessment instruments that librarians can employ.

SURVEY PROCEDURE

The authors used the standard procedure for *CLIP Note* surveys. After the initial proposal and draft of the survey were submitted to ACRL'S *CLIP Notes* Committee for approval, they were mailed to participants in August 2001 and returned through the end of September 2001. Due to a relatively low initial response rate, a second mailing was sent out in October 2001 and responses were accepted through December 2001.

ANALYSIS OF SURVEY RESULTS

GENERAL INFORMATION ON SURVEY RESPONDENTS (Questions #1-7)

Surveys were sent to 293 college and university libraries, of which 158 responded, representing a 54% response rate. The institutions ranged in size from student bodies of 550 (FTE) to 9300 (FTE). Of these institutions, 34% were public, 66% were private. For purposes of analyzing some of the survey responses based on size of institution, the institutions were grouped into the following categories: 1000 or fewer FTE students (14 libraries); 1001-3000 FTE students (88 libraries); 3001-5000 FTE students (30 libraries); and over 5000 FTE students (26 libraries).

INSTRUCTION STAFFING, HOURS, AND SESSIONS (Questions #8-12)

The survey was intended, in this first section, to determine what sort of staffing library instruction required and how many clock hours (that is, 60-minute hours) were required. Further, surveying the number of those hours that represented credit-bearing instruction revealed the number of hours for which the institution received "compensation" (that is, in the form of tuition).

How many librarians are involved in instruction? (Questions #8-9)

The institutions represented by survey respondents employed an average of 7.68 librarians (Question #8), with an average of 5.33 (or 69%) of them doing instruction as some part of their job (Question #9). Of these, most seemed to be full-time employees (that is, not many institutions appeared to rely predominantly on part-timers for their instruction).

The size of the institution did have an effect on the actual number of librarians that did instruction as part of their jobs. What was particularly telling was that the ratio of students to librarians doing instruction was markedly different from smallest to largest institution. In libraries with 1000 students or fewer, the ratio of students to librarians was 431:1; in institutions with 1001-3000 students, 523:1; in institutions with 3001-5000, 890:1, and in institutions with more than 5000 students, 1042:1.

How many hours of instruction are offered in how many sessions? (Questions #10-11)

The average number of library instruction hours taught by librarians was 138 hours (Question #10), making the average number of hours taught by each librarian 26 hours, or a little less than 1 hour (52 minutes) each week if spread out over a 30-week academic year. Further, given the average number of sessions at these institutions (Question #11), the data show that librarians taught an average of 22 sessions each.

The number of sessions taught can identify the average length of an instructional session. Librarians taught an average of 117 sessions for an average of 138 hours, making an average session length 71 minutes.

The number of hours per student also varied by size, with the group of smallest institutions (that is, 1000 and fewer students) offering the most instruction *per student*. Overall, private institutions offered more instruction per student although, in the 3001-5000-student range, the public institutions actually offered more than the private institutions in that range.

How many instructional hours are credit-bearing? (Question #12)

Credit-bearing library instruction accounted for a very small percentage of the total instruction that took place. Of the average number of clock hours taught per year (138 hours), only an average of 19 hours (14%) were taught in credit-bearing classes. One way of looking at this is that most library instruction is not reimbursed through tuition receipts and (presumably) load credit. Instead, it is simply incorporated into the librarians' jobs. The percentage does not seem to be markedly different in public (15%) and private (13%) institutions, nor are the percentages strictly by size. The one notable exception is that, among public institutions of 3001-5000 students, 30% offered credit-bearing instruction, nearly twice the percentage of any other group of institutions.

Several institutions indicated that, while their library instruction did not explicitly bear academic credit, passing the library instruction component was necessary to pass a course in which it was embedded or attached, so that, as one institution mentioned, "passing one was part and parcel of passing the other."

At some institutions, a credit-bearing library instruction course is required for some majors, while offered as an elective ("gen. ed.") for other students.

TYPES AND SCOPE OF LIBRARY INSTRUCTION (Questions #13-17)

The survey was designed to determine the primary types of instruction among responding libraries, how pervasive *required* library instruction was, what the average credit hour requirements were at institutions that have required instruction, and when (at what level) instruction occurred in the various disciplines.

How is instruction delivered? (Question #13)

Overall, four types of instructional methods or formats seemed to predominate, being reported by well over half of the responding libraries: the so-called "one-shot" course-related lecture (150 libraries, or 95%); the orientation/tour (117 libraries, or 74%); the multiple (2-3) session instruction offering (108 libraries, or 68%); and the instruction session that lasts less than a full class period (101 libraries, or 64%). In addition to the one-shot *course-related* lecture, 76 libraries (48%) reported offering one-shot *non*-course-related instruction. The short instructional unit, ranging from less than a class period to 2-3 periods, represented fully two-thirds (67%) of responses to this question.   This no doubt reflects the demand placed on librarians as well as the political realities of trying to offer a significant library instruction component while not adding credit hours (see credit hour issue addressed in Questions #16 and #17) or overburdening students with a requirement that is not reflected on a transcript.

One finding that was a bit surprising was that only 34 libraries (21.5%) used online tutorials, a format that seems to be cost-effective (e.g., less staff time). Among other explanations, this may reflect the value placed on face to face instruction or the lack of technical resources or expertise to create and maintain online tutorials.

There are, of course, myriad varieties of library instruction, many of which were listed in the survey. However, respondents also reported using types of instruction other than those identified in the survey, including hybrids of the listed kinds of instruction. Among the additional forms of delivering library instruction that libraries reported were: research consultations or one-on-one sessions, self-directed tours, hands-on worksheets, and workshops on specific topics (e.g., specific software). Combinations, or hybrids, included library instruction as part of the First Year Experience programs offered at some institutions, and the format described by another institution, which offered a combination of short lecture and individualized help, followed by final discussion of the research process.

Instruction delivery by size of institution (Question #13)

It was thought that institutional size might influence the type or format of instruction offered but, surprisingly, there was little difference. The one-shot, course-related session was the instructional format most frequently reported by libraries in every size range (1000 and under; 1001-3000; 3001-5000; over 5000 FTE students), with 100% of institutions with 3001 and more FTE students reporting offering this type of instruction. The orientation and/or tour was the second- most frequently offered instruction in all but the smallest institutions. The other two predominant instructional formats–the instructional offering of 2-3 class sessions and the unit of less than one full class period–were consistent as well.

Probably the most significant finding when examining type of instruction and institutional size was the increase in the percentage of institutions offering self-directed tutorials and credit courses taught by librarians. While only 17% (at most) of institutions with 3000 students or fewer offered credit courses taught by librarians or self-directed tutorials, 27%-40% of larger institutions (more than 3000 students) offered credit courses and/or self-directed tutorials. The increase in number of credit courses taught by librarians may by explained by an increase in the size of library staffs at those institutions, while the increasing use of self-directed tutorials may represent a less labor-intensive way of providing instruction to large numbers of students. It is clear, at the very least, that larger institutions offered more variety in types of instruction tailored to a range of circumstances.

Required instruction (Question #15)

More than half the libraries surveyed (92 libraries, or 58%) did *not* have required formal instruction for all students (e.g., a freshman library instruction component). Of those that required library instruction (66 libraries, or 42%), no one format was favored. Orientations or tours were the most frequently reported required library instruction component (23 of 66 libraries, or 35%), followed by one-shot, course-related instruction (18 of 66 libraries, or 27%).

There was also significant variety in the scope of the requirements, some requiring only orientation tours, others multiple sessions for all first year students or components in a required course. At some institutions, library instruction was a requirement only for specific majors. One institution indicated that they had a curricular requirement simply that library instruction be taught, which generally meant a one-shot session by a librarian but the session *could* be taught by the course professor. Among the more extensive requirements was the program at Wartburg College, which had an Information Literacy Across the Curriculum (ILAC) requirement, in which library instruction was built into four general education classes and, in addition, required that "each academic department have an information literacy strand built into its major."

Credit hours for instruction (Questions #16-17)

In all, 32 libraries (20%) out of all 158 responding libraries reported offering instruction for academic credit, whether as a curricular requirement (as in 10 libraries, or 6%) or as a credit-bearing elective (27 libraries, or 17%). (Note that 5 of these libraries offered both required and non-required library instruction for academic credit.) Of these, the average number of credit hours required (1.29 credit hours) was significantly lower than the average number of credit hours of instruction offered but not required (2.06 credit hours). The average number of credit hours offered overall (that is, required and non-required) was 1.9 credit hours. Because there was such a small sample of responses to these questions, it is hard to draw conclusions about practices in different types of institutions, and it is feared that the question itself may have been misinterpreted. Nevertheless it seems clear that not much library instruction is being offered for academic credit and, for libraries considering a credit-bearing instructional course, 1-2 credit hours might be an appropriate target.

Discipline-specific instruction (Question #14)

Most of the statistics drawn from this survey did not particularly distinguish among general classes and/or subject-specific classes. It is probably safe to assume that many reflected both general instruction and discipline-specific instruction. Question #14, however, was intended to determine which disciplines included more (or less) library instruction, and whether there was a clearly preferred year in which instruction was given in a particular disciplinary area. It should be noted that, as expected, many comments indicated that when discipline-specific instruction was offered depended on when it was requested.

According to the raw data, the Social Sciences and then Humanities reported the most instruction overall. While the survey did not take into account the possibility that some institutions may not offer programs in certain disciplines, the wide disparity among the instruction reported in these two areas and the others makes it seem safe to say that there was more call for instruction in the Social Sciences and Humanities than in the Natural Sciences, Arts, Health and Medicine, and professional programs.

Overall, the most discipline-specific instruction regardless of discipline was offered in the junior year (the instruction reported across disciplines in the junior year totaled an aggregate of 588). The freshman and sophomore years each had the same aggregate amount (528), with more instruction in the Social Sciences in the sophomore year, and more in the Arts, Humanities, and "other" category in the freshman year.

One interesting finding was the number of institutions that offered instruction at the graduate level. Even allowing for the fact that a number of institutions participating in the survey did not have graduate programs, 55% (87 libraries) responded that they offered instruction to graduate students in the Social Sciences and almost a third (49, or 31%) indicated that they offered instruction to Humanities students at the graduate level. In undergraduate instruction, no clear trends emerged within disciplines. The Arts seemed to slightly prefer instruction at the freshman level, the Social Sciences at the sophomore and junior levels, and Natural Sciences, Health and Medicine, and professional programs at the junior level, while there was no significant difference in the Humanities among the four undergraduate levels.

Interesting among the comments were one institution's more extensive requirement of library instruction for their Honors program, and another institution's indication that library instruction was offered to faculty, too.

CONTENT AREAS COVERED BY LIBRARY INSTRUCTION (Question #18)

An overall survey of library instruction content was intended to reveal not only whether there was fairly common content among libraries (that is, content that a significant percentage deemed worthy of teaching), but also to determine whether librarians actually assessed the content that they taught. The list of content areas supplied in the survey proved to be quite comprehensive, as only a handful of respondents indicated other content areas they taught, usually functional content such as logging onto a computer, using uniprint systems, or using microfilm and fiche.

It was clear that certain content areas were far more common than others. Determining what content most libraries taught *all* students demonstrated what institutions have chosen to emphasize, perhaps because of the value or importance placed on them, or perhaps because of students' difficulty with that content. The top 6 content areas reportedly taught to *all* students were: use of online catalog (83, or 52.5%); use of online indexes (81, or 51%); library services (e.g., reserves) and locations (76, or 48%); selecting appropriate tools for research (72, or 46%); selecting terms and keywords (66, or 42%); and physically locating materials in library (65, or 41%).

While these were the content areas libraries reported most frequently requiring *all* students to learn, they do not represent the overall prevalence of coverage, since, for many content areas, the number of libraries teaching to *all* was significantly lower than the number that taught to at least *some* of their students. Examining the content areas most taught to either *all* or *some* of the students (that is, the content most taught overall; determined by totaling the number of libraries that taught particular content to all *and* to some) is another way of analyzing or determining importance of content. When examined in this way, the following emerged: Again, the use of online catalog was the most frequently taught (156, or 99%), followed by use of online indexes (155, or 98%). The next four most frequently taught content areas were: distinction between popular and scholarly sources (154, or 97%); library services (e.g., reserves) and locations (153, or 97%); selecting appropriate tools for research (151, or 96%); and selecting terms and keywords (150, or 95%). Overall, then, there was a consistency in the selection of content areas to be taught: library catalog and online indexes, selecting appropriate research tools and terms, and library services.

The content areas that were taught by the fewest number of libraries, regardless of how calculated, were: the ethical and economic implications of information (e.g., plagiarism, copyright), and the nature and process of scholarly publication.

ASSESSMENT OF INFORMATION LITERACY (Questions #19-21)

Once having established the current status of instruction at surveyed institutions, it was then possible to address the issue of assessment of library instruction. Question #19 ascertained, in the most general terms, the amount of formal assessment being done overall. Ninety-four of the 158 responding libraries (or 59%) did at least some sort of formal assessment after library instruction.

How is assessment done? (Question #20)

The most frequently used assessment tool among the 94 libraries that assess instruction was the multiple choice or short answer test (used by 47 libraries, or 50%). Other methods of assessing student knowledge used by at least 30% of respondents who assess were: assignments other than papers (32 libraries, or 34%); and inclusion as part of a professor's exam (29, or 31%). The numbers of attitudinal assessments used were lower than expected. Twenty-seven libraries (29% of assessing libraries) used an attitudinal assessment that was part of a general library survey; 34 libraries (36% of assessing libraries) used a separate attitudinal survey after library instruction. As one might expect, respondents' comments reflected the fact that not all assessment was done using the same type of instrument, and that the type of assessment used sometimes depended on the professor and the course. Among the "other" assessment instruments reported were hands-on lab exercises and "one-minute assessment papers with subjective responses."

Respondents also made it clear that in some instances, grading was done by the librarian, in others by the professor, and in at least one instance, a respondent noted that the "librarian grades the bibliographic portion and the teacher grades for content." Self-assessment and assessment by student peers were also mentioned.

What content is assessed most (and least) frequently? (Question #21)

So, *what* was it that librarians assessed most? And was it the same content that librarians most often taught?

Among the content areas there were no areas that the 94 assessing libraries overwhelmingly favored assessing and, in fact, there was no content area in which more than 22% assessed *all* students' competency. The five content areas in which the 94 assessing libraries most often assessed all students' competency were: using the library online catalog and using online indexes (each by 21 libraries, or 22%); selecting appropriate tools and reading or deciphering citations (each by 20 libraries, or 21%); and distinguishing between popular and scholarly sources (18, or 19%).

The five content areas least likely to be assessed were: the nature and process of scholarly communication (5 libraries, or 5%); primary and secondary sources (6 libraries, or 6%); plagiarism (7 libraries, or 7%); and copyright, truncation and proximity, and paper indexes (each by 8 libraries, or 8.5%). This may be explained by the difficulty of developing adequate or practical ways of testing competencies in these areas or simply the level of importance placed on them.

Again, as with determining libraries' priorities in terms of *teaching* content, the level of importance placed on assessing content can be determined by the number of libraries that assessed that content the most overall (by calculating the sum of how many either assess all or some students' competency). Competency in using online indexes proved to be assessed most frequently (56 out of 94 libraries, or 60%), followed by use of the online catalog (54, or 57%), selecting appropriate tools (49, or 52%), and distinguishing between scholarly and popular sources. And not surprisingly, copyright, plagiarism, scholarly publication, and truncation/wildcard/proximity were again the least likely to be tested.

And how does what is taught compare with what is assessed? (Questions #18 and #21)

Of course, these statistics only reflect how one content area compares to another in terms of how frequently it was assessed. Another important point of comparison is between what was *taught* and what was *assessed*. Such comparison reveals that the most frequently taught areas were, by and large, also the most frequently assessed. Use of the online catalog, use of online indexes and selecting appropriate tools appeared among the most taught and most assessed. The distinction between scholarly and popular resources seemed to be prevalent as well. But while the use of library services and selection of keywords and terms were among the content areas most taught, they were not among the most assessed.

Further, and more revealing, is how little was assessed in general. For example, while (in Question #18), 83 libraries reported teaching use of the library online catalog to all students and 81 taught the use of online indexes, only about a quarter of them in each case assessed their students' competency in these two areas. The third most represented area, teaching appropriate tools, was *taught* to all students by 72 libraries, but only 20 libraries (or 28% of those that taught it) reported *assessing* all students.

For further comparison of what is taught with what is assessed, see Tables I and II on the following pages.

TABLE I: CORRELATION BETWEEN WHAT IS FORMALLY TAUGHT AND WHAT IS FORMALLY ASSESSED (FROM QUESTIONS #18 AND #21 OF THE SURVEY)

This table presents a composite or overview of what is taught and/or assessed.

	A. Do not teach or assess		B. Teach only		C. Teach and Assess		D. Assess Only	
	#	%	#	%	#	%	#	%t
a) Research Process	7	4.43%	107	67.72%	44	27.85%	0	0.00%
b) Knowledge of Library/Terminology	21	13.29%	96	60.76%	40	25.32%	1	0.63%
c) Library Services	5	3.16%	110	69.62%	43	27.22%	0	0.00%
d) Selecting: appropriate tools	6	3.80%	104	65.82%	47	29.75%	1	0.63%
e) Selecting: appropriate resources	12	7.59%	103	65.19%	43	27.22%	0	0.00%
f) Scholarly vs. popular sources	4	2.53%	108	68.35%	46	29.11%	0	0.00%
g) Primary and secondary sources	14	8.86%	119	75.32%	25	15.82%	0	0.00%
h) Selecting terms and keywords	7	4.43%	110	69.62%	40	25.32%	1	0.63%
I) Keyword vs. subject headings	11	6.96%	112	70.89%	35	22.15%	0	0.00%
j) Boolean operators	10	6.33%	111	70.25%	36	22.78%	1	0.63%
k) Truncation, wildcard, proximity	15	9.49%	121	76.58%	22	13.92%	0	0.00%
l) Use of library catalog	2	1.27%	102	64.56%	54	34.18%	0	0.00%
m) Use of paper indexes	27	17.09%	99	62.66%	32	20.25%	0	0.00%
n) Use of online indexes	3	1.90%	99	62.66%	56	35.44%	0	0.00%
o) Use of other ref/research tools	11	6.96%	111	70.25%	36	22.78%	0	0.00%
p) Use of web	12	7.59%	108	68.35%	38	24.05%	0	0.00%
q) Web site evaluation	9	5.70%	111	70.25%	38	24.05%	0	0.00%
r) Call numbers	20	12.66%	103	65.19%	35	22.15%	0	0.00%
s) Physically locating materials in library	12	7.59%	108	68.35%	38	24.05%	0	0.00%
t) Citations: reading/deciphering	21	13.29%	95	60.13%	42	26.58%	0	0.00%
u) Citations: accurately citing	34	21.52%	87	55.06%	35	22.15%	2	1.27%
v) Economic implications	59	37.34%	75	47.47%	23	14.56%	1	0.63%
w) Ethical implications	48	30.38%	86	54.43%	23	14.56%	1	0.63%
x) Nature/process of scholarly publication	53	33.54%	85	53.80%	17	10.76%	3	1.90%
y) Other	138	87.34%	13	8.23%	1	0.63%	6	3.80%

A. Libraries that *neither taught nor assessed any* students (that is, they checked neither "all" nor "some" for teaching; and they checked neither "all" nor "some" for assessing).

B. Libraries that *taught at least some* students but *did not assess any* (that is, they indicated they taught either "all" or "some" students, but did not indicate that they assessed this content at all).

C. Libraries that *taught at least some* students and that *assessed at least some* students (that is, the sum of those that checked that they taught either "all" or "some" *and* checked that they assessed either "all" or "some").

D. Libraries that *did not teach any* students but *assessed at least some* students (that is, they did not indicate they taught either "all" or some" students; but they did indicate that they assessed either "all" or "some").

TABLE II: WHAT <u>ALL</u> STUDENTS ARE TAUGHT AND WHAT <u>ALL</u> STUDENTS ARE ASSESSED ON (FROM QUESTIONS #18 AND #21 OF THE SURVEY)

	A. Do not teach or assess		B. Teach only		C. Teach and Assess		D. Assess only	
	#	%	#	%	#	%	#	%
a) Research Process	99	62.66%	47	29.75%	11	6.96%	1	0.63%
b) Knowledge of Library/Terminology	103	65.19%	42	26.58%	11	6.96%	2	1.27%
c) Library Services	82	51.90%	61	38.61%	15	9.49%	0	0.00%
d) Selecting: appropriate tools	83	52.53%	55	34.81%	17	10.76%	3	1.90%
e) Selecting: appropriate resources	106	67.09%	40	25.32%	10	6.33%	2	1.27%
f) Scholarly vs. popular sources	102	64.56%	38	24.05%	16	10.13%	2	1.27%
g) Primary and secondary sources	133	84.18%	19	12.03%	5	3.16%	1	0.63%
h) Selecting terms and keywords	90	56.96%	51	32.28%	15	9.49%	2	1.27%
I) Keyword vs. subject headings	98	62.03%	46	29.11%	13	8.23%	1	0.63%
j) Boolean operators	106	67.09%	36	22.78%	14	8.86%	2	1.27%
k) Truncation, wildcard, proximity	130	82.28%	20	12.66%	6	3.80%	2	1.27%
l) Use of library catalog	74	46.84%	63	39.87%	20	12.66%	1	0.63%
m) Use of paper indexes	137	86.71%	13	8.23%	8	5.06%	0	0.00%
n) Use of online indexes	76	48.10%	61	38.61%	20	12.66%	1	0.63%
o) Use of other ref/research tools	125	79.11%	23	14.56%	9	5.70%	1	0.63%
p) Use of web	121	76.58%	24	15.19%	11	6.96%	2	1.27%
q) Web site evaluation	125	79.11%	18	11.39%	12	7.59%	3	1.90%
r) Call numbers	109	68.99%	34	21.52%	14	8.86%	1	0.63%
s) Physically locating materials in library	90	56.96%	51	32.28%	14	8.86%	3	1.90%
t) Citations: reading/deciphering	111	70.25%	27	17.09%	14	8.86%	6	3.80%
u) Citations: accurately citing	128	81.01%	18	11.39%	10	6.33%	2	1.27%
v) Economic implications	144	91.14%	6	3.80%	5	3.16%	3	1.90%
w) Ethical implications	139	87.97%	12	7.59%	7	4.43%	0	0.00%
x) Nature/process of scholarly publication	148	93.67%	5	3.16%	4	2.53%	1	0.63%
y) Other	151	95.57%	6	3.80%	1	0.63%	0	0.00%

This table reports only the "All students" responses in survey Questions #18 and #21 (that is, those libraries that indicated that they taught "All" students particular content, assessed "All" students on particular content, or both taught and assessed "All students"). Column C is of the most significance, indicating the number of libraries that taught *and* assessed all students (that is, they checked "all" in Question #18 *and* "all" in Question #21).

THE ACRL STANDARDS AND LIBRARY INSTRUCTION (Questions #22-24)

How are the ACRL Standards used in instruction programs? (Questions #22-23)

Because the ACRL's *Information Literacy Competency Standards for Higher Education* (2000) is a relatively recent document, this portion of the survey was designed to determine the extent to which libraries address the standards in their information literacy program and how many libraries are assessing student competency in the same areas. The five broad ACRL standards were used to ascertain this data. (Some standards were abbreviated for the purpose of this survey.)

> 1. Student determines nature and extent of information need.
> 2. Student accesses needed information effectively and efficiently.
> 3. Student evaluates quality and usefulness of information and incorporates information into knowledge base and value system.
> 4. Student uses information effectively to accomplish specific purpose.
> 5. Student understands the economic, legal and social issues surrounding use of information.

The number of libraries that reported instructing *all* of their students in the standards' content was much lower than those that instructed *all* or *some* of their students. Standard 2 received the highest response of 59 institutions (37%) that reported teaching it to *all* students while 41-45 of the respondents (26-28%) reported teaching *all* students Standards 1, 3 and 4. Standard 5 had a significantly lower response rate of 14 institutions (9%), perhaps explained by the fact that, for many institutions, "all" meant "first year students," and issues covered in Standard 5 might be better understood by upper class students.

When combining the respondents who addressed Standards 1-4 with either all *or* some of their students, it became clear that support for the standards was widespread. Out of 158 respondents, 133-141 of the institutions (84-89%) addressed standards 1-4 with *all* or *some* of their students. Standard 5 was addressed the least, but still, 94 respondents (59%) reported teaching about the economic, legal and social issues of information use to at least *some* of their students.

Having determined how many institutions included concepts found in the standards in their *instruction*, it was interesting to see how many of those institutions reported *assessing* student competency in relation to the standards. The number of libraries that reported *assessing* student learning of the standards' concepts was dramatically lower than the number that *taught* standards, with a high of 56 libraries (35%) assessing for Standard 2 followed by 40-46 libraries (25-29%) assessing competencies for Standards 1, 3 and 4. Again, Standard 5 had the lowest response with only 29 of the respondents (18%) reporting that they assessed student competency. For all but Standard 5, then, institutions assessed less than half of the standards that they taught. (Standard 5 was assessed 41% less.)

Size of Institutions and the ACRL Standards (Questions #22-23)

Teaching and assessing the ACRL standards' concepts did not differ, on the whole, based on institutional size. However, a few findings did stand out. Among libraries that reported teaching standards to *all* students, a higher percentage of institutions with 1,000 and under FTE students reported teaching all standards than the percentage of larger institutions. Within this group of smaller schools, teaching of Standards 3 and 4 was significantly higher with a difference of 36% (Standard 3) and 23% (Standard 4) above institutions in the larger categories. One explanation for this considerable difference could be that it is less complicated logistically to reach all of a smaller student body than it is for institutions with enrollments above 1,000 FTE.

The size of institution also made a significant difference in assessment. Institutions with enrollments of 3001-5000 FTE reported a higher frequency of assessing *all* or *some* students' competencies in all five standards than other size categories. In particular, libraries in this group reported assessing standards 3 and 4 16% and 12% more (respectively) than any other size category (42-47% vs. 21-31%).

Implementation of the ACRL Information Literacy Standards (Question #24)

Finally, the survey attempted to ascertain when, or if, institutions were implementing the ACRL information literacy standards. Not surprisingly, only 8 of 152 responding libraries (5%) had already systematically incorporated the standards into their information literacy programs although 48 (or 32%) reported being in the process of implementation at the time the survey was completed. Somewhat surprising, however, were the 26 libraries (17%) that had *no* immediate plans to include any of the standards in their instruction program. The positive news is that 115 libraries (76%) were in various stages of planning to use the standards, i.e., they had either partially incorporated them (32%), were reviewing them for inclusion (23%), or planned to address the issue in the next 2-3 years (21%). Clearly, the majority of respondents are, or will be, implementing the ACRL standards into their information literacy programs.

ASSESSMENT OF LIBRARY PERSONNEL (Questions #25-28)

This section of the survey was intended to ascertain who teaches library instruction, whether those instructing were evaluated and, if so, by whom. If librarians were being evaluated, the authors wanted to find out what sorts of assessment instruments were being used and what criteria were being applied.

Who does library instruction? (Question #25)

Out of 158 respondents, library instruction at the majority of institutions was taught by professional librarians *only* (112 institutions, or 71%). Fewer institutions reported that they provided teaching by professional librarians and teaching faculty (42 institutions, or 27%) as did those that used both professional librarians and "other library staff" (22 institutions, or 14%). A small number of institutions (9, or 6%) paired professional librarians with other campus professionals such as computing staff. Under "other," a few respondents commented that they used "other library staff" as assistants in the classroom only.

Are the library instructors given performance evaluations of library instruction sessions? (Question #26)

Over half of the institutions (89, or 56%) did *not* give performance evaluations while 67 institutions (42%) did evaluate library instructors. Several respondents noted that because librarians did not have faculty status at their institutions, evaluations were only used as feedback for the instructors themselves, and not for purposes of promotion.

On what are evaluations based? (Question #27)

Results from this question are calculated as a percentage of the 67 institutions that reported giving performance evaluations in Question #26. Respondents were asked to check *all* forms of evaluation that applied. By far, the largest number of libraries (49, or 73%) used student evaluation forms. Next in line were written or oral faculty feedback (35, or 52%) and formal classroom observations by other librarians (24, or 36%). Fourteen libraries (21%) used formal classroom observation by faculty as a criterion for evaluation with only 8 (12%) reporting that they used student performance. The prevalence of student evaluation tools most likely reflects the tools' undemanding nature compared to tools assessing student learning.

What criteria or areas are measured? (Question #28)

Once again, results were tabulated out of the 67 responses to Question #26. Four criteria, or areas, that were most often used to assess library instruction were: knowledge of material (62, or 93%), teaching ability (58, or 87%), organization (55, or 82%), and appropriateness of the teaching for the class (54, or 81%). Three other criteria received from 31-35 responses (46-52%): visual aids, in class student responsiveness, and timeliness (currency) of the material. Student performance again had the least number of respondents (17, or 25%). Respondents' comments also indicated other criteria such as "respect for students," clarity, and presentation style.

CONCLUDING COMMENTS FROM RESPONDENTS (Questions #29-30)

Comments on library instruction or information literacy at responding institutions (Question #29)

Although there was a wide range of remarks from the 55 institutions that provided comments in this section, most frequent were comments such as "we need some pressure from 'above' or outside [the] institution," while others specifically mentioned needing more faculty cooperation and stronger administrative support. One librarian expressed his/her frustration about institutional support this way: "I'm a voice 'crying in the wilderness' [about information literacy] – there are no hearers."

It was heartening to find that a number of librarians reported that they *had* received helpful support from the faculty and administration, and that they *did* have strong programs in place as formal parts of the curriculum. Two comments are representative: "Just last week our faculty voted to include information literacy as a goal of our year-long freshman course...." And, "The library is becoming more and more included in campus decisions about curriculum and programs, providing an excellent opportunity to promote information literacy."

Finally, it should be noted that, while only 8 libraries reported directly using the ACRL standards, several respondents commented on the fact that their information literacy programs had already addressed *parts* of the standards' content.

Comments on assessment of library instruction or information literacy at responding institutions (Question #30)

Of the 41 institutions providing comments for this question, many referred to plans or hopes for the future in the area of assessment, with a few who expressed a desire to know "how other libraries are assessing student performance." Other respondents identified the difficulty of doing assessment in the setting of "one-shot" instruction sessions where no opportunity was given to do formal assessment of student learning. Additional comments described specific assessment methods or tools being used.

CONCLUSION

It seems clear from the survey results that, while a substantial amount of formative assessment has been done, summative assessment, which "measures actual learning," still lags behind and, while making strides, has yet to become the norm. Further, since very little library instruction is being offered for academic credit or is being required for graduation, students are not getting significant credit for what they have learned. As accrediting agencies and librarians themselves make further progress in advancing the need for information literacy, the assessment of both student competency and instructor effectiveness will surely become more rigorous and more common; summative evaluation will become more widespread; and even campuswide required library instruction will become the expectation.

WORKS CITED

American Library Association Presidential Committee on Information Literacy: Final Report, 1989. American Library Association. 27 Mar. 2002. <http://www.ala.org/acrl/nili/ilit1st.html>

Breivik, Patricia Senn. "A Vision in the Making: Putting Libraries Back in the Information Society." *American Libraries*, 16, no. 10 (1985): 723.

Iannuzzi, Patricia. "We are Teaching, But Are They Learning: Accountability, Productivity, and Assessment." *Journal of Academic Librarianship* 25, no. 4 (1999): 304-5.

Information Literacy Competency Standards for Higher Education, 2000. Association of College & Research Librarians. 8 Mar. 2002. <http://www.ala.org/acrl/ilcomstan.html>.

Rabine, Julie L. and Catherine Cardwell. "Start Making Sense: Practical Approaches to Outcomes Assessment for Libraries." *Research Strategies* 17, no. 4 (2000): 319-35.

Rader, Hannelore. "From Library Orientation to Information Literacy." *What is Good Instruction Now? Library Instruction for the 90s.* Ed. Linda Shirato. Ann Arbor: Pierian Press, 1993. 25-28.

Riddle, John S. and Karen A. Hartman. "'But Are They Learning Anything?' Designing an Assessment of First Year Library Instruction." *College & Undergraduate Libraries* 7, no. 2 (2000): 59-69.

Seamans, Nancy H. "Information Literacy: A Study of Freshman Students' Perceptions, with Recommendations." Ph.D. diss., Virginia Polytechnic Institute and State University, 2001. <http://scholar.lib.vt.edu/theses/available/etd-05142001-104550/unrestricted/Seamans.pdf> (20 March 2002).

Stewart, Sharon Lee. "Assessment for Library Instruction: the Cross/Angelo Model." *Research Strategies* 16, no. 3 (1998): 165-74.

SELECTED BIBIOGRAPHY

SELECTED BIBLIOGRAPHY

Ackerson, Linda G. and Virginia E. Young. "Evaluating the Impact of Library Instruction Methods on the Quality of Student Research." *Research Strategies* 12, no. 3 (1994): 132-44.

Baker, Ronald L. "Evaluating Quality and Effectiveness: Regional Accreditation Principles and Practices." *Journal of Academic Librarianship* 28, no. 1-2 (2002): 3-7.

Cameron, Lynn. "Assessment of Library Skills (at James Madison University)." *What is Good Instruction Now? Library Instruction for the 90s."* Ed. Linda Shirato. Ann Arbor: Pierian Press, 1993. 47-50.

Carter, Elizabeth W. "'Doing the Best You Can with What you Have:' Lessons Learned from Outcomes Assessment." *Journal of Academic Librarianship* 28, no. 1-2 (2002): 36-41.

Colborn, Nancy Wootton and Rosanne M. Cordell. "Moving from Subjective to Objective Assessments of your Instruction Program." *Reference Services Review* 26, no. 3-4 (1998): 125-37.

Dunn, Kathleen. "Assessing Information Literacy Skills in the California State University: A Progress Report." *Journal of Academic Librarianship* 28, no. 1-2 (2002): 26-35.

Fourie, Ina and Daleen Van Niekerk. "Using Portfolio Assessment in a Module in Research Information Skills." *Education for Information* 17, no. 4 (1999): 333-52.

Greer, Arlene, et al. "Assessment of Learning Outcomes: a Measure of Progress in Library Literacy." *College & Research Libraries* 52, no. 6 (1991): 549-57.

Iannuzzi, Patricia. "We are Teaching, But Are They Learning: Accountability, Productivity, and Assessment." *Journal of Academic Librarianship* 25, no. 4 (1999): 304-5.

Information Literacy Competency Standards for Higher Education, 2000. Association of College & Research Librarians. 8 Mar. 2002. <http://www.ala.org/acrl/ilcomstan.html.

Lindauer, Bonnie Gratch. "Comparing the Regional Accrediation [*sic*] Standards: Outcomes Assessment and Other Trends." *Journal of Academic Librarianship* 28, no. 1-2 (2002): 14-25.

Maki, Peggy L. "Developing an Assessment Plan to Learn about Student Learning." *Journal of Academic Librarianship* 28, no. 1-2 (2002): 8-13.

Maughan, Patricia Davitt. "Assessing Information Literacy Among Undergraduates: A Discussion of the Literature and the University of California-Berkeley Assessment Experience." *College & Research Libraries* 62, no. 1 (2001): 71-85.

Rabine, Julie L. and Catherine Cardwell. "Start Making Sense: Practical Approaches to Outcomes Assessment for Libraries." *Research Strategies* 17, no. 4 (2000): 319-35.

Riddle, John S. and Karen A. Hartman. "'But Are They Learning Anything?' Designing an Assessment of First Year Library Instruction." *College & Undergraduate Libraries* 7, no. 2 (2000): 59-69.

Samson, Sue. "What and When do They Know? Web-based Assessment." *Reference Services Review* 28, no. 4 (2000): 335-42.

Seamans, Nancy H. "Information Literacy: A Study of Freshman Students' Perceptions, with Recommendations." Ph.D. diss., Virginia Polytechnic Institute and State University, 2001. <http://scholar.lib.vt.edu/theses/available/etd-05142001-104550/unrestricted/Seamans.pdf> (20 March 2002).

Stewart, Sharon Lee. "Assessment for Library Instruction: the Cross/Angelo Model." *Research Strategies* 16, no. 3 (1998): 165-74.

Williams, Janet L. "Creativity in Assessment of Library Instruction." *Reference Services Review* 28, no. 4 (2000): 323-34.

Young, Virginia E. and Linda G. Ackerson. "Evaluation of Student Research Paper Bibliographies: Refining Evaluation Criteria." *Research Strategies* 13, no. 2 (1995): 80-93.

SURVEY RESULTS

CLIP NOTE Survey on Assessment
in College Library Instruction Programs

Name of person completing survey:_____

Title of person completing survey:_____

Name of institution:_____

General Data

Note: All figures requested in this section (questions 1-12) are for Fall 2000 or Fiscal Year 1999-2000.

1. Size of institution (FTE Students) **avg. = 2978.24; range = 550 - 9300***(158 responses)*

2. Institution is: **54** Public **104** Private   *(158 responses)*

3. Number of full-time equivalent (FTE) faculty
   avg. = 181; range= 45 - 543   *(158 responses)*

4. Approx. number of book volumes, excluding bound periodicals in your library
   avg.= 259,226; range = 50,000 - 1,200,000   *(157 responses)*

5. Approximate number of current print periodical subscriptions
   avg. = 1354; range= 183 - 9379   *(158 responses)*

6. Approximate total budget for your library   *(151 responses)*
   avg. = 1,293,760; range = 80,000 - 4,930,000

7. Approximate total materials expenditures for your library   *(154 responses)*
   avg. = 483,508; range = 50,283 - 1,940,000

8. Number of FTE librarians   **avg. = 7.68; range = 2 - 22**   *(158 responses)*

9. Number of librarians doing library instruction as some *part* of their jobs
   avg. = 5.33;   range= 1-20   *(156 responses)*
   full-time librarians **avg. = 4.74; range = 0 - 16**
   part-time librarians **avg=.54; range = 0 - 8**

10. Total number of library instruction *class hours* (including partial hours) taught per year
(credit and non-credit) (e.g., 30-minute class = .5 hours)   *(133 responses)*
   avg=138.45; range = 0 - 1050

11. Total number of library instruction sessions taught per year   *(157 responses)*
   avg. = 117.43; range = 0 - 1207

12. How many of those hours are creditbearing (e.g., academic credit, graduation credit)?
   avg=19.19;   range = 0 - 270   *(154 responses)*

Library Instruction: Type and Scope

This section (questions 13-17) attempts to get a general, overall picture of library instruction on your campus, the amount of library instruction *all* students get, and the academic credit given.

13. Which of the following describe the type of *formal* library instruction (e.g., not Ref. desk) offered at your institution (*check all that apply*):   *(158 responses)*

101	a) Library instruction session less than full class period in duration
150	b) One-class, course-related library instruction session (the "one shot" lecture)
76	c) One-class, NON-course-related library instruction session (the "one shot" lecture)
117	d) Orientation/tour
108	e) Multiple sessions (e.g., 2-3 class sessions) but not a credit course
35	f) Credit course taught by a librarian
10	g) Credit course team taught by a librarian and a disciplinary faculty member
34	h) Self-directed tutorial (e.g., online)
0	i) No formal library instruction is offered
17	j) Other_____

14. Question regarding discipline-specific library instruction: If you offer library instruction for specific subjects or courses, at what level(s) does this occur *(check all that apply)*:

(157 responses)

	FR	SO	JR	SR	Grad. Level
a) Humanities (History, Literature, Religion, etc.)	127	121	125	120	49
b) Social Sciences (Educ., Anthro., Psych., Econ., etc.)	109	129	135	103	87
c) Natural Sciences	81	81	93	76	31
d) Health and Medicine	58	58	74	60	40
e) Arts	82	74	78	64	27
f) Professional programs (Engineering, Business)	54	56	73	62	57
g) Other: _____	17	9	10	8	12

15. Which of the following describe an institutional (e.g., curricular) <u>requirement</u> made of <u>all</u> students (*check all that apply*):   *(158 responses)*

4	a) Library instruction session less than full class period in duration
18	b)One-class, course-related library instruction session (the "one shot" lecture)
7	c) One-class, NON-course-related library instruction session (the "one shot" lecture)
23	d) Orientation/tour
11	e) Multiple sessions (e.g., 2-3 class sessions) but not a credit course
8	f) Credit course taught by a librarian
2	g) Credit course team taught by a librarian and a disciplinary faculty member
9	h) Self-directed tutorial (e.g., online)
92	i) No library instruction is required for all students
18	j) Other_____

16. If credit-bearing library instruction is <u>required</u>, how many credit hours?
      <u>avg. = 1.29; range = .4 - 3</u>   *(10 responses)*

17. If credit-bearing course is <u>offered but not required</u>, how many credit Hours?
      <u>avg. = 2.06; range = 1 - 6</u>   *(27 responses)*

Library Instruction: Content

This section (question 18) attempts to determine what content is most common among libraries by identifying which elements are taught to *all* students. Distinctions in the columns below (i.e., between "all" and "some") recognize that some institutions do not have a library instruction requirement for *all* students or that some material is covered in *some* but not *all* library instruction.

18. Which of the following do you formally teach in your library instruction *(check all that apply)*:

(158 responses each)

Teach ALL students	Teach SOME students	
58	93	a) research process
53	83	b) knowledge of library and research terminology
76	77	c) library services (e.g., reserves) and locations
72	79	d) selecting: appropriate tools (e.g., indexes)
50	96	e) selecting: appropriate resources (e.g., format, date)
54	100	f) distinction between scholarly and popular sources
24	121	g) primary and secondary sources
66	84	h) selecting terms and keywords
59	88	i) keyword vs. subject headings
50	97	j) boolean operators
26	117	k) truncation, wildcard, proximity
83	73	l) use of/searching in: Library catalog
21	110	m) use of/searching in: paper indexes
81	74	n) use of/searching in: online indexes
32	115	o) use of/searching in: other ref. or research tools (online and/or paper)
35	111	p) use of/searching in: web
30	119	q) web site evaluation
48	90	r) call numbers
65	81	s) physically locating materials in library
41	96	t) citations: reading/deciphering bibliographic information in indexes, catalogs, etc.
28	94	u) citations: accurately citing using standard style guides (e.g., APA, MLA)
11	87	v) economic implications of information (eg. copyright)
19	90	w) ethical implications of information (eg. plagiarism)
9	93	x) nature and process of scholarly publication
7	7	y) other (please specify):_____

Assessment of Student Information Literacy: Type and Scope

19. Is students' knowledge or understanding *formally* assessed (that is, through quiz, bibliography assessment, survey, etc.) after library instruction? *(158 responses)*
   Yes **21**   No **64**   Some but not all **73**

(If no, skip to question 22)

20. If so, how is formal student assessment done? *(check all that apply)*:

   47   a) Multiple choice/short answer quiz or exam
   5   b) Essay quiz or exam
   29   c) Included in course professor's quiz/exam
   6   d) Face to face interview (or oral exam)
   27   e) Record of research process (e.g., research log, reflective writing on process)
   28   f) Assessment of bibliography used in paper
   17   g) Assessment of complete paper and bibliography
   32   h) Assignments other than papers
   27   i) Attitudinal assessment: as *part of general survey* of library users' attitudes
   34   j) Attitudinal assessment: *separate survey* pertaining to library instruction
   ~~k) deleted this question No formal assessment~~
   21   l) Other:_____

Assessment of Student Information Literacy: Content

21. Do you formally assess student competency in *(check all that apply)*:   *(158 responses)*

Assess ALL students	Assess SOME students	
12	32	a) research process
13	28	b) knowledge of library and research terminology
15	29	c) library services (e.g., reserves) and locations
20	29	d) selecting: appropriate tools (e.g., indexes)
12	31	e) selecting: appropriate resources (e.g., format, date)
18	28	f) distinction between scholarly and popular sources
6	19	g) primary and secondary sources
17	24	h) selecting terms and keywords
14	22	i) keyword vs. subject headings
16	21	j) boolean operators
8	14	k) truncation, wildcard, proximity
21	33	l) use of/searching in: Library catalog
8	24	m) use of/searching in: paper indexes
21	35	n) use of/searching in: online indexes
10	26	o) use of/searching in: other ref. or research tools (online and/or paper)
13	25	p) use of/searching in: web
15	23	q) web site evaluation
15	20	r) call numbers
17	21	s) physically locating materials in library
20	22	t) citations: reading/deciphering bibliographic information in indexes, catalogs, etc.
12	25	u) citations: accurately citing sources using standard styles guides (e.g., APA, MLA)
8	16	v) economic implications of information (eg. copyright)
7	17	w) ethical implications of information (eg. plagiarism)
5	15	x) nature and process of scholarly publication
1	6	y) other (please specify):_____

➔➔➔➔**Please submit documents (or URLs) assessing competency in any or all of the above.**

The ACRL Standards and Library Instruction

ACRL's *Information Literacy Competency Standards for Higher Education* (2000) provides "a framework for assessing the information literate individual." Following are the 5 broad information literacy standards from the ACRL document.

This section (questions 22-24) attempts to determine the extent to which libraries are incorporating the standards into the content of their library instruction and assessing student competency.

22. Please check each BROAD standard that you attempt to *address* at some point in your information literacy program: *(158 responses)*

Instruct ALL students	Instruct SOME students	
45	97	a) Student determines nature and extent of information needed
59	82	b) Student accesses needed information effectively and efficiently
44	93	c) Student evaluates quality and usefulness of information and incorporates information into knowledge base and value system.
41	92	d) Student uses information effectively to accomplish specific purpose
14	80	e) Student understands the economic, legal and social issues surrounding use of information

23. Now, please check each BROAD standard for which student competency is formally *assessed*:
(158 responses)

Assess ALL students	Assess SOME students	
14	26	a) Student determines nature and extent of information needed
19	37	b) Student accesses needed information effectively and efficiently
11	34	c) Student evaluates quality and usefulness of information and incorporates information into knowledge base and value system.
15	31	d) Student uses information effectively to accomplish specific purpose
6	23	e) Student understands the economic, legal and social issues surrounding use of information

24. Please indicate if/when you plan to implement the ACRL information literacy standards into your program: *(152 responses)*

8	a) we have already systematically incorporated them;
48	b) we are currently incorporating them, but have not done so fully;
35	c) we are currently reviewing them for inclusion;
32	d) we hope to address this in the next 2-3 years;
3	e) we hope to address this in the next 4-6 years;
26	f) we have no immediate plans to include them.

Assessment of Library Instruction Personnel

This section (questions 25-28) is intended to survey and ascertain what sorts of assessment is being done of the personnel involved in library instruction.

25. Who does library instruction *(check all that apply)*:   *(158 responses)*

    112   a) professional librarians only;
     22   b) professional librarians and other library staff;
     42   c) professional librarians and teaching faculty;
      9   d) professional librarians and other campus professionals (e.g., computing staff);
      5   e) other_____(please specify)

26. Are the library instructors given performance evaluations of library instruction sessions?
    Yes **67**   No **89**   *(156 responses)*

    (If Yes, then complete questions 27 and 28. If No, you have completed the survey.)

27. On what are evaluations based *(check all that apply)*:   *(67 responses)*
     49   a) student evaluation forms
      8   b) student performance
     24   c) formal classroom observation by other librarians
     14   d) formal classroom observation by other faculty
     35   e) other faculty feedback (written or oral)
      8   f) other:_____

28. What criteria or areas are assessed *(check all that apply)*:   *(67 responses)*

     58   a) teaching ability
     62   b) knowledge of material
     31   c) timeliness (currency) of material
     17   d) student performance
     55   e) organization
     31   f) inclass student responsiveness
     35   g) visual aids
     54   h) appropriateness for class
      9   i) other:_____

➜➜➜➜**Please submit documents (or URLs) that assess the competency and effectiveness of instructors in your library instruction program.**

<u>**Comments**</u>

29. Please use the space provided to make further comments *on library instruction or information literacy* at your institution:

30. Please use the space provided to make further comments *on assessment* of library instruction or information literacy at your institution:

➜➜➜➜**Please make sure to submit documents (or URLs) assessing information literacy and/or library instruction.**

DOCUMENTS: *Pre-Tests*

Assessment Of Familiarity With Library Terms

Can you match the description with the correct term?
Write the description number next to the correct library term below.

1. Description of a source you consult.
2. Shelving code that keeps books about similar subjects near each other.
3. Source for a newspaper articles. Newspaper clippings arranged together on microfiche.
4. Index for finding citations for articles in scholarly periodicals.
5. Service for borrowing books and articles Delta does not own.
6. Periodical written to satisfy the interests and reading abilities of the general public.
7. Periodical written by and for specialists, often reporting research information.
8. List of periodical titles that the Delta Library owns.
9. Source for finding books and other materials in library collections in our geographic area.
10. Standardized terms used to categorize information logically.
11. Search term that can be retrieved from anywhere in an indexed field, e.g., title, subject, abstract.
12. Index for finding citations for popular magazine articles.
13. Styles of writing and citing research papers.
14. Comments about a source, usually critical or explanatory.
15. Online indexes to over 60 databases.
16. Online index and full-text to a mix of sources.
17. Index to U.S. publications.
18. Index to materials cataloged by world libraries.
19. Index to professionally evaluated World-Wide Web sites.
20. Paragraph that summarizes the content of a journal or magazine article.

_____ Citation   _____ MLA and APA

_____ Journal   _____ FirstSearch

_____ GPO CAT/PAC   _____ Keyword

_____ Delta College holdings list   _____ Magazine

_____ Interlibrary loan   _____ Abstract

_____ WorldCat   _____ Newsbank Index

_____ VALCAT catalog   _____ Reader's Guide to Periodical Literature

_____ NetFirst   _____ Social Science Index

_____ Subject heading   _____ Annotation

_____ Library of Congress call number   _____ Infotrac

Franklin & Marshall College Library
Information Literacy Survey

Please complete this survey to help the librarians better understand first-year student knowledge of a college library and to better tailor our teaching to your needs.

1. The best place to look for background or introductory information on a topic (such as "astronomy") is:

a) A library catalog
b) A reference book
c) A scholarly journal

2. A primary source contains:

a) Research on the first primates
b) Data gathered from a primary election
c) Information produced in the original historical context

3. To find the most current information on a topic, it is best to consult:

a) Books
b) Journal articles
c) Encyclopedias

4. You are assigned to research the topic "stem cells" by starting with general research sources, then proceeding to more specific sources. Which of the following sequences best illustrates this progression:

a) Books ➡ Journal articles ➡ Encyclopedias
b) Journal articles ➡ Encyclopedias ➡ Books
c) Encyclopedias ➡ Books ➡ Journal articles

5. A bibliography is a list of:

a) Information sources
b) Geographic sites
c) Libraries

6. The best way to find out if the library has a book that you need is to:

a) Look around for the book on the shelves
b) Look up the book in a catalog
c) Find the title in a bibliography

7. What are the main concepts or ideas in the following research question:

"What are the effects of increasing global warming on oceans?"

a) global warming, oceans
b) increasing, global warming, oceans
c) effects, global warming, oceans

8. Information found on the Internet may not be appropriate for scholarly research because:

a) Scholars do not put information on the Internet
b) Most information on the Internet is free for anyone to use
c) Not all information on the Internet is authoritative

9. A professor requires you to read 3 scholarly articles from 3 different sources about the presidential election of 2000. It is best to start looking for these articles using:

a) An Internet search engine (Google, Yahoo, etc.)
b) The library catalog
c) A journal index

10. Read the following research question and determine which of the following statements would retrieve the **best** results from a database search:

"What was the role of women in the Civil War?"

a) role and Civil War
b) women and Civil War
c) role or women or Civil War

11. Documenting a source is necessary only when you are using a direct quotation from it.

a) true   b) false

12. There is scholarly information on the Internet available only through a paid subscription by a library.

a) true   b) false

13. I do not need to question or evaluate the information I find in library resources.

a) true   b) false

14. Students do not need to be concerned about copyright issues because educational uses of information are exempt from copyright rules.

a) true   b) false

15. Electronic journals always feature the exact same content as print journals.

a) true   b) false

During your high school career how often did you use a computerized index of journal articles or books to find information on a topic?

never   once   2-5 times   more than 5 times

During your high school career how often did you have to write a research paper which required you to use sources beyond those used in your class?

never   once   2-5 times   more than 5 times

Name:_____ Year: FR_____ SO_____
(We request your name only for data gathering purposes, to avoid duplication. Your name and responses will not be seen by your professor.)

Lynchburg College
Knight-Capron Library _____ INFORMATION LITERACY PRETEST

Description: Tests basic information literacy skills Instructions: Follow the instructions for each question. Click on the "submit" button at the end of the test to record your answer. Upon completion of the test you will be given your raw score in number of points for correct answer and your percentage of correct answers. You have 45 minutes to complete this test.   Good luck.

1.   From the following list select those items that can be found in LION, the online catalog. (15pts)

❏ Which journals have articles on a particular topic.

❏ Which books are in the library and where they are located.

❏ Full text on internet conference proceedings.

❏ Which issues of a magazine the Library owns.

❏ Which items are on Reserve for a course.

❏ Which textbooks are required for courses at Lynchburg College.

Questions 2 through 5 refer to the following entry from **LION**, the online catalogue:

Call Number:	STACKS ON THE SECOND FLOOR LB2343.32 .R67 1992	STATUS:checked In
Record#	451360	
Author:	Rosenberg, Ellen.	
Title:	College Life/Ellen Rosenberg.	
Publisher:	New York: Penguin Books, 1992.	
Descript.: xvi, 333: 23cm.		
Subjects:	College student orientation – United States	
	College students -- counseling of.	
	College students – Mental health.	
	College students – Health.	
	College students – Social conditions.	

2. If you were searching for this book by author, and you typed Ellen Rosenberg in the search box, would this record be retrieved? (2 pts)

❏ True

❏ False

3. This book would NOT be found using a subject keyword search for "College Life? (2 pts)

❏ True

❏ False

4. This book could be found using a Subject Exact or Subject List search for which of the following? (2 pts)

- ❑ College students - orientation
- ❑ College orientation
- ❑ College student orientation
- ❑ College life

5. Where is this book located in the library? (2 pts)

- ❑ With the other books by Ellen Rosenberg
- ❑ On the first floor with other books on college life.
- ❑ On the second floor next to book #451359
- ❑ On the second floor in the section with call numbers beginning with LB2343.32.

6. Put the following book call numbers in the order they would appear on the library shelves by matching each call number with its rank number. (10 pts)

- ❑ E48 .B67
- ❑ HD117 .R4
- ❑ HQ117 .N39
- ❑ HC4682 .E5
- ❑ HV481 .B68
- ❑ D375 .D4
- ❑ DA113 .C3
- ❑ E475 .B6

A. 1st
B. 2nd
C. 3rd
D. 4th
E. 5th
F. 6th
G. 7th
H. 8th

7. You have been assigned a paper on a topic you are not familiar with and need to do some research. If your strategy is to find general background information, then detailed specific case studies and finally recent research studies or analyses from the last year on your topic, which of the following groups of resources would be the most logical sequence to follow. (5 pts)

- ❑ Scholarly journal articles, a general encyclopedia, books on the topic
- ❑ A general encyclopedia, scholarly journal articles, books on the topic
- ❑ Books on the topic, scholarly journal articles, a general encyclopedia
- ❑ A general encyclopedia, books on the topic, scholarly journal articles

8. A bibliography contains which of the following: (5 pts)

❏ details about a particular individual's life
❏ statistical charts and graphs
❏ citations for sources of information on a particular topic
❏ Names and addresses of government officials

9. Roommatism: how to live with others without killing yourself. (includes related article) (College 1994) (Cover Story) Dan Zevin. Rolling Stone Oct 20, 1994 n693 p131(2)

Based on the above citation from the periodical index Expanded Academic ASAP, which of the following is FALSE? (5 pts)

❏ The author of this article is Dan Zevin
❏ This article appears in the October 20th, 1994 issue of Rolling Stone.
❏ This article appears on page 131, column 2.
❏ this article appears in issue number 693 of Rolling stone.
❏ The title of this article is "Roommatism:how to live with others without killing yourself."

10. Match the following citations with the type of information source each represents. (18 pts)

_____Hamilton, James T. "Does Viewer Discretion PromptAdvertiser Discretion? The Impact of Violence Warningson the Television Advertising Market.." in Television Violence and Public Policy. Hamilton, James T.(ed.). Ann Arbor, MI:U of Michigan Press. (1998):213-66.

A. Newspaper article

_____Rovinelli, Lea and C. Whissell. "Title Emotion and Style in 30-Second Television Advertisements Targeted at Men, Women, Boys, and Girls." Perceptual & Motor Skills 86, no.3 (1998): 1048-1050.

B. An article from a scholarly journal

_____Schmidt, Rosemarie and Joseph F. Kess. Television Advertising and Televangelism: Discourse Analysis of Persuasive Language. Amsterdam: Benjamins. (1986).

C. A chapter from a book of essays

D. An article from a popular magazine

_____Murray, John P. Impact of Televised Violence. <www.ksu.edu/ humec/impact.htm > 3 November, 2001 (January 30, 2002.)

E. A book on the topic

_____Begley, Sharon. "Talking From Hand to Mouth." Newsweek, 15 March 1999, 25.

F. An article or document from an

Internet Web site.

_____Saltus, Richard. "Survey Connects TV Fare, Child Behavior." The Boston Globe, 21 March, 2001: A1.

11. The following is a list of journal, magazine and newspaper articles take from an online periodical index. Match the part of a citation or the type of citation from the list that follows with descriptions on the right. (18 pts)

1. Is College Dangerous?(heath hazards of college life) Richard P. Keeling. Journal of American College Health, Sept 2001 v50 i2 p53.

2. College requires students to clean their own bathrooms. Curriculum Review, March 2001 v40 i7 pS4

3. "Freshman-Year Experience." Ronald Roach. Black Issues in Higher Education, Feb 19,1998 v14 n26 p30(2).

4. Live from college it's ... a messy room. (growing popularity of Web cams in dormitories) Abby Ellin. The New York Times Jan 9, 2000 pED7(L)

5. "31 Fun Reasons To Go To College." Marc Goodman. Rolling Stone, Oct 11, 2001 i879 p68(4).

Match

_____ growing popularity of Web cams in

dormitories in #4

_____ "Is College Dangerous?" in article #1

_____ Ronald Roach in article #3

_____ The number 68 in article #5

_____ Journal of American College Health in article #1

_____ v40 i7 in article #2

A. Article title

B. Name of scholarly journal

C. Page number where the beginning of

the article is found.

D. Name of popular magazine

E. Article description added by index

F. The volume and number of the issue

where the article is found.

G. Author of the article

12. Of the following, which is/are NOT a primary source for a paper on the U.S. involvement in the Vietnam conflict of 1961-1973? (8 pts)

❑ Transcriptions of President Lyndon Johnson"s tape recordings of conversations with his Secretary of State, Dean Rusk, published in 2002.

❑ Philip Caputo's book " A Rumor of War." published 19

❑ Commander of U.S. forces, William S Westmorland's memoir, "A Soldier Reports."

❑ A New York Times article from April 30, 1993 on the 30th anniversay of the evacuation of Saigon that ended U.S. involvement.

Title: American Demographics

Library/Collection/Call Number	Format	Status
1. Lynchburg College	--	Active
Recent issues are in current periodical room		
Previous issues are bound or on microformat.		
vol.22, no.1 (Jan., 2000) – vol.24, no2 (Feb., 2002)		
2. Lynchburg College	Microfiche	Inactive
Periodical on Microfiche		
vol. 19 (1997) –vol.21 (1999)		
Lynchburg College	Microfilm	Inactive
Periodical on microfilm		
vol.14 (1992) – vol.18 (1996)		

13. Based on the above entry from LION, the online catalog, the volume 12, no.2, Feb.1990 issue of the periodical is: (5 pts)

❑ shelved in the Current Periodical Room.

❑ available on microfiche in the MicroFormat Room.

❑ not owned by Lynchburg college

❑ Shelved with the other bound volumes of this periodical.

14. For a paper on single sex colleges, you used a book that you found in the library about women college students. When you started typing your bibliography, you couldn't find the paper that had the information you needed to cite this book. You had already taken the book back and the library is currently closed. You log on to the online catalog, but you can't remember the author's name or the full title. You know the word "romance" was in the title plus the word "education" or "educated". Which of the following searches would be the fastest way to find the record for the book? (5 pts)

❑ Subject search for "college education"

❑ Call number search for LC (letter combination that begins call numbers for books on higher education)

❑ Title List search for "education" or "educated" and "romance."

❑ Title keyword search for "romance, " "educat?

❑ Title keyword search for "romance"

15. The Library has a section where professors may place materials for restricted in-house use or short term loan. This is known as what? (5 pts)

❑ Reference

❑ Special Collections

❑ Reserves

❑ Circulation check-out

16. If you are using LION, the online catalog to find a book in the library, match the most efficient search on the right to find the items in the list to the left. (20 pts)

If you are looking for :

_____ A book by John Lennon

_____ "In His Own Write" by John Lennon

_____ A book about John Lennon

_____ A book about the Beatles

Possible ways to search:

A. Title Key Word search for "His Write."

B. Subject List search for "Lennon, John,"

C. Title Key Word search for " The Beatles."

D. Author Search for "Lennon, John."

E. Title List Search for "In His Own."

F. Subject List search for "Beatles."

17. Which of the following are examples of plagiarism? (10 pts)

❑ Jim writes a paper based on information he finds in CQ Researcher and several journal articles. He cites each in the bibliography of his paper.

❑ Helen is writing a paper on the Pro-choice movement. She cuts and pastes a section
❑ from the Website of The National Organization of Women. Since this is her only source she doesn't attach a bibliography citing it.

❑ Gene copies a paragraph from an article in Sports Illustrated for his paper on pro-football marketing. Because he doesn't use the entire article he doesn't include a citation to this article in his bibliography

❑ Brian consults the Encyclopedia Britannica when he begins researching a paper on Thomas Jefferson. Even though the encyclopedia lists among Jefferson's in his paper accomplishments the authorship of the Declaration of Independence, when Brian uses this item he does not need to cite Britannica in his bibliography.

❑ Jennifer uses several passages from a chapter of a book on child abuse for a Sociology paper. She changes the order of the original sentences and paraphrases parts of them.

For Questions 18 through 20 first read the following excerpt from a journal article. Then answer the questions that follow based on your reading

---

Rauf, Don. "Life on Campus" *Careers & Colleges* 21 no. 4 (2001): 10-13.

Your fellow classmates may be stressed out. A I record-breaking 30.2 percent of freshmen say they are "frequently overwhelmed" by all they have to do, according to an annual survey of 404,667 new college freshmen, conducted by UCLA's "This is a reflection of an increasingly fast-paced society, made more so by computers and other media," says the survey's director, UCLA assistant education professor Linda J. Sax. "Students feel more competition; they're applying to more colleges than ever before; they're worried about having to work during college. That can be overwhelming."

Women tend to spend more time than men studying, doing volunteer work, participating in student organizations and tending to housework or child-care responsibilities. Men, on the other hand, spend more time than women exercising or playing sports, watching television, partying or playing video games.

Compared to a year ago, new undergraduates are not as interested in becoming "an authority," and "recognition from colleagues" ranked at an all-time low. In general, students care less about status, but more than 70 percent are interested in being very well-off financially and raising a family.

As far as personal habits, you can expect almost half of the fall class to be drinking beer at least occasionally, but only 10 percent are smokers. Freshmen today are more tolerant of gay rights--14 years ago, 50 percent of freshmen believed "it is important to have laws prohibiting homosexual relationships"; today that figure is down to 27 percent. The UCLA survey also shows a rise in freshman opposition to the death penalty--31.2 percent say it should be abolished compared to 24.1 percent in 1998.

---

18. Which of the following possible Subject Headings for this article would you use in a database search to find articles of a similar nature. (5 pts)

- ☐ Students
- ☐ College life - freshmen
- ☐ UCLA Higher Education Research Institute.
- ☐ Study Habits
- ☐ Alcohol Use

19. Which of the following Boolean search sentences would be most likely to retrieve this rticle and other relevant articles? (5 pts)

- ☐ Habits AND college students OR college freshmen
- ☐ College campuses AND (students OR freshmen)
- ☐ Students AND surveys NOT High school
- ☐ Student life AND (colleges OR universities)

20. If you were doing a 10 page term-paper on the topic covered in the article, which of the following online periodical indexes would be a logical place to start your search (5 pts)

- ☐ A World Wide Web search engine
- ☐ ERIC - An index that contains abstracts of education resources, including journal articles,
- ☐ books, theses, conference papers, standards and guidelines
- ☐ Lexis-Nexis - a database covering a wide range of news, business, legal and reference information
- ☐ JSTOR -Provides electronic access to the full-text of older back issues of core scholarly journals in the humanities, sciences, and social sciences.

Maryville College
Maryville, Tennessee
Information Literacy Competency Inventory

Gender:_____

According to the American Library Association, information literacy is *"a set of abilities requiring individuals to recognize when information is needed and have the ability to locate, evaluate, and use effectively the needed information."* At Maryville College, information literacy skills are incorporated across the curriculum. This inventory is designed as a starting point to measure competencies set forth by the Association of College and Research Libraries. THIS INVENTORY WILL NOT BE GRADED. It will be used to identify areas in the curriculum that need further development.

Circle the letter to the response that best answers the following. There is only one correct answer for each question.

1. **Which of the following is a characteristic of scholarly journals?**

   a. contains glossy pictures and advertisements
   b. reports news events in a timely manner
   c. contains a literature review within the articles
   d. provides an author's opinion about a controversial event

2. **Which of the following titles would be considered the title of a popular magazine?**

   a. Journal of Higher Education
   b. Newsweek
   c. Economic Review
   d. American Journal of Political Science

3. **Which of the following is a primary source?**

   a. a literary text, such as The Scarlet Letter by Nathanial Hawthorne
   b. books written about The Scarlet Letter
   c. journal articles written about The Scarlet Letter
   d. dissertations written about The Scarlet Letter

4. **Conducting a survey would be an example of?**

   a. independent research
   b. secondary research
   c. primary research
   d. historical research

5.   **Which of the following contains an example of truncation?**

a.   dogs and kittens
b.   dogs or cat
c.   kitt* and dogs
d.   cat not kitt

6.   **Which of the following contains a Boolean operator?**

a.   cars into trucks
b.   cars and trucks
c.   cars before truck
d.   cars behind trucks

7.   **When using a library's online catalog for finding books, a subject search on John Grisham would find?**

a.   magazine articles written by the author
b.   books written about the author and his works
c.   newspaper and magazine articles about the author and his works
d.   books written by the author

8.   **To find books written by Margaret Mead, you would use a library's online catalog to do a/an:**

a.   title search
b.   author search
c.   subject search
d.   performance search

9.   **The following....**

Adams, Margot. "Eudora Welty: Southern Woman." <u>Southern Voices</u>:
    <u>An Anthology</u>.   Ed. Tamara Kingsley. New York: Random House,
    1998. 35 – 41.

    is a bibliographic citation for a:

a.   journal article
b.   personal interview
c.   world wide web site
d.   book chapter

10. **The following….**

Mathews, Lawrence. "Urban Development and Growth." American
        Spectator. May 1998: 23 – 30.

is a bibliographic citation for a:

a.   book
b.   subject encyclopedia
c.   journal article
d.   world wide web site

11. **A bibliographic citation for a World Wide Web site should contain:**

a.   information about external links
b.   the date the site was accessed
c.   members of the organization
d.   contact information

12. **Which of the following best represents a Uniform Resource Locator (URL)?**

a.   http://www.millennium2000.org/events/
b.   658.009 L653d
c.   smith@prodigy.com
d.   HG 7402.3 L8555

13. **Which of the following is an important criterion that you should use to evaluate information found on a web site?**

a.   file size
b.   authority
c.   location
d.   bandwidth

14. **If you are writing a paper on animal rights and you use information from a web site produced by PETA—the People for the Ethical Treatment of Animals, which web site evaluation criterion should you consider?**

a.   location
b.   bias
c.   currency
d.   links

15. **To find peer-reviewed or refereed information on a topic of interest, you would most likely look for:**

    a.   websites on your topic
    b.   personal interviews with experts on your topic
    c.   journal articles on your topic
    d.   newspaper articles on your topic

16. **Which of the following is the name of a periodical database?**

    a.   InfoTrac
    b.   Yahoo
    c.   Alta Vista
    d.   Lycos

17. **Which of the following is the name of an Internet Search Engine?**

    a.   Lexis-Nexis Universe
    b.   JSTOR
    c.   http://www.whitehouse.gov/
    d.   Google

18. **Periodical databases will lead you to:**

    a.   books about people, places and events
    b.   magazine and journal articles
    c.   web sites containing magazine and/or book articles
    d.   reference books on a specific subject

19. **Not giving proper acknowledgement for another writer's work, thought, or argument is known as:**

    a.   originalism
    b.   citation
    c.   referencing
    d.   plagiarism

20. **If you collect images from the Word Wide Web and then compile these images into a web site, paper, or display for a class project, gained permission from the owner to use these images and have given proper credit to the author, you have:**

    a.   committed plagiarism
    b.   destroyed intellectual content
    c.   complied with copyright law

BASIC SKILLS SURVEY
Fall 2000

1. NAME:

[   ]

2. EMAIL ADDRESS:

[   ]

3. Status:
○ First-Year Student
○ Sophomore
○ Junior
○ Senior

4. Which of the following situations would indicate a need for in-depth information? Check all that apply.
☐ A pedestrian prepares to cross the street in a busy intersection in a foreign country.
☐ A worker in a high-rise glass office building must determine if it is raining.
☐ A student must choose between two colleges with the same tuition costs.
☐ A newspaper reader must decide between two editions of the same newspaper.
☐ Two companies of the same size in the same city offer a college graduate a high-paying position.

5. One difference between a reference book and circulating book is:
○ Reference books are used less often
○ Circulating books are much more expensive
○ Reference books cannot be taken out of the library
○ Circulating books are always classified as fiction

6. Journals differ from magazines in that:
○ Journals are published periodically
○ Journals are important sources of academic research
○ Journals are available by subscription
○ Journals have volume numbers.

7. Yahoo! is primarily:
○ a commercial directory
○ a nonprofit organization
○ a search engine
○ where all Websites in the known universe live.

8. My high school library provided Internet access.
○ True
○ False

9. Plagiarism is the same thing as the fair use policy.
○ True
○ False

10. The kind of information found on the Internet is the same kind found in academic libraries.
○ True
○ False

11. The hardest part of writing a research paper is:

12. Last year the most important thing I learned about information resources was:

13. I can define the terms *citation*, *bibliography*, *index*, and *database*.
○ Yes
○ No
○ Not Sure

14. The U.C. Library offers interlibrary loan service.
○ True
○ False

Submit | Reset

[http://www.uchaswv.edu/library/instruct/skill.html]

Questions from Your Friendly Reference Librarian, Celita DeArmond
Thank you for your time. Your answers will help me plan instruction for your class.

Using the Library Catalog The library catalog will tell you what a library owns--books, magazines and journals, newspapers, videos, recorded music, etc. The UTSA Libraries catalog's name is UCAT.

1. Have you ever used an online (computerized) library catalog to locate items at any library?
___ yes, many times   ___ a few times   ___no, never   ___not sure

---

1a. If you have used a library catalog, were you able to locate items that fit your information need?
_____yes, always
_____most of the time
_____sometimes
_____no, never

1b. Share any **questions** you have about library catalogs or **difficulties** you have experienced while searching a library catalog:

_____
_____
_____

2. Here is a *description* of an item that was found by looking in UCAT, the UTSA Libraries catalog. Take a look and then answer the questions below:

AUTHOR:	Luchetti, Cathy, 1945-
TITLE:	"I do!" : courtship, love, and marriage on the American frontier : a glimpse at America's
	romantic past through photographs, diaries, and journals, 1715-1915
EDITION:	1st ed.
PUBLISHED:	New York: Crown Trade Paperbacks, c1996.
SUBJECTS:	Courtship--United States--History.
	Marriage--United States--History.
	Frontier and pioneer life--United States.
	United States--Social life and customs.

LOCATION:	CALL NUMBER:	STATUS:
Main Stacks	HQ 801 .L828 1996	not checked out

2a. What **type** of item is this?   ___ journal   ___book   ___newspaper   ___recording   ___not sure

2b. When was this item **published**? _____

2c. If you wanted to find other items about the same topic, what other **key words** or **phrases** could you use to search UCAT?

_____
_____

3. In general, do you feel comfortable locating books by call number in the library? (any library)

Using Periodical Indexes/Abstracts Periodical indexes/abstracts are the tools you use to locate individual articles in magazines, journals and newspapers. An abstract (summary) of the article will usually accompany the citation (address) of the article. Indexes/abstracts can be either in print or online.

4. **Have you ever used an index/abstract to help you locate articles in a magazine, journal or newspaper?**

____ yes, many times   ____ a few times   ____no, never   ____not sure

4a. If you have searched for articles, were you able to locate items that fit your information need?

_____yes, always
_____most of the time
_____sometimes
_____no, never

4b. Share any **questions** you have about finding periodical articles or **difficulties** you have experienced while using an index/abstract to find periodical articles:

_____
_____
_____

General/Internet Questions

5. **What level are you in college?** ___Freshman ___Sophomore ___Junior ___Senior __Graduate___Transfer

6. **Have you ever attended a library class before?** ___ yes   ___no

6a. If you have attended a library class, did you find that it was helpful to you?   ___ yes   ___no

6b. Share specific reasons why or why not you felt the class was helpful:

_____
_____
_____

7. **Have you ever surfed the Internet/World Wide Web?**

____yes, lots of times   ____yes, a few times   ____no, never

7a. If you have surfed the Internet/WWW, what kinds of things did you use the Internet for?

____email   ____chat rooms   ____research   ____just browsing around
____other:_____

7b. How do you personally determine if an Internet source is **reliable** to use for your information need?

8. **What topics or events are of interest to you for use in library research? Which academic subjects Interest you?**

9. **Share some specific questions or concerns about the UTSA Libraries or library research in general:**

DOCUMENTS:
Pre- and Post-Test Sets

DataMine/I
Spring, 2001

1. What is difficult for you about using the library?

2. If you want to find a book on the history of hip-hop, where would you look?

___Databases page off of the Emerson College Library Webpage
___Yahoo!
___Library Catalog
___Books in Print

3. Assume you are writing a paper on the culture and history of hip-hop. What source might not be useful as you research your paper?

___Perkins, William Eric., ed. *Droppin' Science: Critical Essays on Rap Music and Hip Hop Culture*. Philadelphia: Temple University Press, 1996.
___Kenon, Marci. "Incoming: A Guide To New Hip-Hop Releases." *Billboard* 1 April 2000: 60.
___Samuel, Allison, N'Gai Croal, David Gates and Alisha Davis. "Battle for the Soul of Hip-Hop." *Newsweek*, 9 Oct., 2000. 58-66.
___Robinson, Ruth Adkins. "Hip-Hop History." *Billboard*, 4 Dec. 1999: 38-41.

4. If you are searching through an online tool for articles on *history of hip-hop*, what search terms would help you find the most complete list or articles?

___Hip-hop
___African-American AND music
___Hip-hop AND history
___(Hip-hop OR rap) AND history

5. If your professor tells you to find a scholarly article on hip-hop history, what would be the best place to look?

___The Web
___The Library Catalog
___Lexis-Nexis Academic Universe
___Academic Search Elite

6. What would be most useful for you to learn during this session?

DataMine/II
Spring, 2001

1. What's one thing that you learned in the library.

2. If you have a citation to a specific article in a journal, where might you start to look for it?

___Search Yahoo!
___Look for the title of the article in Lexis-Nexis
___Search for title of the journal in the Library Catalog
___Search WorldCat

3. If you cannot find the journal in the library, where else might you look?

___List of Print and Online Periodicals
___Dogpile
___Library Catalog
___Books in Print

4. If you search for, "**hip-hop AND history,**" in the Library Catalog and you don't find useful sources, what might your next step be?

___Search for **hip-hop**
___Search for **African-American and Music and History**
___Search through Ask Jeeves
___Search for **(hip-hop OR rap) AND history**

5. If your professor tells you to find a scholarly article on hip-hop history, what would be the best place to look?

___The Web
___The Library Catalog
___Lexis-Nexis Academic Universe
___Academic Search Elite

6. What's your top reason for using the library?

Cardinal Quiz (Pre-Assessment)

The Cardinal Quiz is designed to help you determine which parts of the quest will be the most useful to you. It also will assist the librarians in deciding which areas they should concentrate on during library instruction sessions.

Students in INST 100, 105 and 110 are required to complete this assessment prior to using the tutorial.

Name:

Course Name and Number, i.e. INST 105:

Professors Name:

Librarian's Name:

1. The numbers PN 1997 .B743 and RC388 .M9 1990 are both

    ❑   Library of Congress call numbers

    ❑   Dewey Decimal call numbers

    ❑   not call numbers at all

2. A bibliography is

    ❑   a book about a person

    ❑   a book of drawings or charts

    ❑   a list of references or citations

3. Search strategy involves

    ❑   planning your approach to searching for information on a subject

    ❑   using an encyclopedia to find information on a subject

    ❑   starting your research by going to a magazine likely to have an article on your topic

4. The *Library of Congress Subject Headings* books

    ❑ list books located in the Library of Congress in Washington, DC

    ❑ indicate which subject headings are used in the online catalog

    ❑ indicate the location of books in the Courtright Memorial Library

5. Libraries offer a variety of computerized databases. The search phrase below which would retrieve the **MOST** records is

    ❑ cognition and emotion

    ❑ cognition or emotion

    ❑ cognition not emotion

6. Courtright Memorial Library's online catalog is called

    ❑ Cardinal Nest

    ❑ Otternet

    ❑ OPAL

7. The Courtright Memorial Library's online catalog DOES NOT contain records for

    ❑ individual journal articles

    ❑ magazines or journals

    ❑ videos

    ❑ books

8. In the Courtright Memorial Library, the most recent issues of magazines or journals are

    ❑ located on the first floor with new books

    ❑ shelved together with older issues of journals

    ❑ located on yellow shelving units at the top of the 2nd floor stairs

9. To obtain citations to recent magazine or journal articles on "Poverty," you would use

    ❑ the online catalog

    ❑ Periodical Abstracts

    ❑ e-mail

10. To obtain assistance in using the library

    ❏ ask at the reference desk

    ❏ ask a friend

    ❏ don't ask anyone; find it on your own

11. A journal (or periodical or magazine) is probably popular if: it is published weekly; it has advertising, particularly for consumer goods; and the articles are short

    ❏ True

    ❏ False

12. A journal (or periodical or magazine) is probably scholarly if: the author's credentials are listed to identify his/her expertise; there are footnotes and long bibliographies; there is an abstract at the beginning of the article; and the article is based on original research.

    ❏ True

    ❏ False

13. Materials from other libraries can be requested through using OPAL, Ohiolink, and/or Interlibrary Loan.

    ❏ True

    ❏ False

References (or citations) to published materials appear in a variety of formats. Look at the following citations (questions 14 – 17) and decide whether they refer to a book or to a journal/magazine article.

14. Reuther, R. (1979). Consciousness-raising at Puebla. Christianity and crisis, 39, 77-80.

    ❏ Book

    ❏ Journal/Magazine Article

15. Austin, B. (1991). Pathogens in the environment. New York: Blackwell Scientific.

    ❏ Book

    ❏ Journal/Magazine article

16. Hudson, C. (1995). Ethology of the South-eastern Indians. New York: Garland.

    ❑ Book

    ❑ Journal/Magazine Article

17. Bamberger, M. (1998, July 13). The pride of Peoria. Sports Illustrated, 19, 15.

    ❑ Book

    ❑ Journal/Magazine Article

18. I attended the Friday night Library New Student Orientation in September during the year I was a Freshman (i.e. 2001 – 2001: A Library Odyssey; 2000 – Around the World in 80 Pages; 1999 – Dr. Seuss; 1998 – Night with the Haunts; 1997 – Alien Adventure; 1996 and 1995 – Murder Mystery)?

    ❑ Yes If so, which year? [＿＿＿＿＿＿＿＿＿＿＿]

    ❑ No

Comments about the event. What did you like or dislike?

[ ]

19. I am a:

    ❑ Freshman

    ❑ Sophomore

    ❑ Junior

    ❑ Senior

    ❑ Graduate Student

    ❑ Other

[Submit]

Please press the Submit button to continue with the Cardinal Quest. Thank you.

[http://www.otterbein.edu/resources/library/libpages/otterquest/Otterquest.htm]

Otter Quiz (Post-Assessment)

Please complete the Otter Quiz after you have used the tutorial. Your professor may ask that you complete it as part of an assignment. If so, please answer the questions and when completed click on the submit button below. Or, if requested to do so by your professor, print it off and turn in a completed paper copy.

Name:

Course Name and Number, i.e. INST 105:

Professor's Name:

Librarian's Name:

1. The Courtright Memorial Library uses several different call number schemes to organize materials. What system is used for the **majority** of books and videos housed in the library?

   ❑ Dewey Decimal

   ❑ Library of Congress (LC)

   ❑ Sudoc

2. When you are deciding on a topic to use for a research paper or speech, the best way to focus your topic would be to: Write down any questions you can think of regarding the topic; Think of specific terms which cover the topic; or Think of synonyms which match your topic.

   ❑ True

   ❑ False

3. When doing a search using a computerized resource, it is often a good idea to use Boolean logic. This involves:

   ❑ Using the words, AND, OR, NOT between terms

   ❑ Typing a question, i.e. When was the U.S. Civil War?

   ❑ Organizing your search in a logical fashion.

4. At the Courtright Memorial Library, the word OPAL refers to:

   ❑ An expensive gem

   ❑ An online catalog

   ❑ The name of the College's network

5. The Courtright Memorial Library's does **NOT** include bibliographic information (author, title, etc.) for:

   ❑ Books

   ❑ Magazines

   ❑ Journal Articles

   ❑ Videos

   ❑ Pamphlets

6. The best way to search for periodical (or magazine or journal) articles is to:

   ❑ Browse through the individual titles

   ❑ Use of microfiche or microfilm machine

   ❑ Use an index (either paper or computerized)

   ❑ Use OPAL or Ohiolink

7. Your professor may indicate to you that you need to use only scholarly publications. Which title listed might meet this requirement:

   ❑ Time

   ❑ Journal of Marriage and the Family

   ❑ American Heritage Magazine

   ❑ Physics Today

8. A good way to increase the number of resources you can find on your topic is to:

   ❑ Ask friends

   ❑ Search the Internet

   ❑ Use a bibliography or works cited

   ❑ Ask a librarian

9. Are the following LC call numbers in the correct order, as they would be on the shelf: N 7525 .V3 1980; N 7740 .H35 1994; NA 31 .B83 1998; NA 31 .B9 1906; NA 7325 .N5?

   ❑ Yes

   ❑ No

10. In order to most effectively use a database's subject searching capability, it is a good idea to:

   ❑ Use a dictionary, such as Webster's Collegiate Dictionary

   ❑ Use the same terms you used in a keyword search

   ❑ Use a database thesaurus or subject heading resource, like LC Subject Headings

11. MLA and APA are:

    ❏ Medical associations

    ❏ Periodical titles

    ❏ Style manuals for help with citations

12. I attended the Friday night Library New Student Orientation in September during the year I was a Freshman (i.e. 2001 – 2001: A Library Odyssey; 2000 – Around the World in 80 Pages; 1999 – Dr. Seuss; 1998 – Night with the Haunts; 1997 – Alien Adventure; 1996 and 1995 – Murder Mystery)?

    ❏ Yes If so, which year? [＿＿＿＿＿＿＿＿＿＿＿]

    ❏ No

Comments about the event. What did you like or dislike?

[   ]

13. I am a:

    ❏ Freshman

    ❏ Sophomore

    ❏ Junior

    ❏ Senior

    ❏ Graduate Student

    ❏ Other

[Submit]

Please press the Submit button to continue. Thank you for using the tutorial.

[http://www.otterbein.edu/resources/library/libpages/otterquest/Otterquest.htm]

DOCUMENTS : *Assignments*

General Assignments
Choosing and Focusing Topic
Identifying Sources on a Topic
Evaluating/Comparing Sources
Finding Articles
Scholarly vs. Popular Periodicals
Web Searching and Evaluation

Name:_____

Due date:_____

InfoTech/Library
OPAC Assignment
#1

Open a web browser
Enter the web address www.catawba.edu
Select library from the drop down menu
Click on the link to the Pleiades-Catawba College OPAC
Click on the link for Local Catalog

1. Perform a Keyword Search using the term **abortions**
   How many entries did you retrieve?_____

2. Under Keyword limit the search to only **Circ** items and search the term **abortions**
   How many entries did you retrieve?_____

3. Under Heading Search, do a subject search on the term **abortion** as a subject. (*hint remove the limit*)
   Select and Open a Heading related to the term listed above.
   List the exact Heading that you opened:
   _____
   How many titles are listed under this Heading?_____
   Select the first entry and give the following information if listed
   Author_____
   Title_____
   Primary Material_____
   Location_____
   Call Number_____
   Status_____
   Is there a Table of Contents for this title?   **Yes   No**

4. Perform an author search for the following writer: **E E Cummings**
   List one Heading for this author_____
   How many titles are listed under this Heading?_____

5. Perform a journal title search for the journal Education Economics and give the following information.
   Primary Material_____
   Location_____
   Call Number_____

Georgia Southwestern State University

UNIV1000 Library Exercise

Your Instructor _____ Date _____ Your Name _____

If you need assistance, please remember that library personnel are here to help you.

I. Using *GIL*, the library's online catalog, locate a **BOOK** on the topic of «**subject**».

    A.   What is the title of the book?_____

    B.   What is the location and full call number of the book? _____

    C.   On which floor of the library is the book shelved? _____

II. From the same list, find a **GOVERNMENT PUBLICATION** on the same topic.

    A.   What is the title of the publication? _____

    B.   What is the full call number of the publication? _____

    C.   On which floor of the library is the publication shelved? _____

III. In *MLA Bibliography* (a GALILEO database), find an article about «**author**».

    A.   What is the title of the article? _____

    B.   Author of the article? _____

    C.   Title of the journal? _____

    D.   Date of the article? _____

    E.   Volume number? _____

    F.   Page numbers? _____

    G.   Using GIL or the Serials printout, find in which format we own the *specific article* you identified.

        bound (or unbound recent issue) _____ microfiche _____ microfilm _____

IV. Multiple choice. Please put an **X** in the blank next to the correct answer.

    A.   In GIL, you need to know *exactly* which book you are looking for in order to do this kind of search.

        _____ title

        _____ command

        _____ subject

    B.   Which collection is located on the second floor of the library?

        _____ main collection (circulating books)

        _____ government documents

        _____ reference

C.   If a book is "checked out" will it be on the shelf?

    _____   yes

    _____   no

D.   Which GALILEO database is a good starting point for most researchers who are looking for journal articles?

    _____   Academic Search Premier (at EBSCOHost)

    _____   Grove Dictionary of Art

    _____   GeorgiaNet

E.   When looking for reliable scholarly research, the *least* reliable source of information is probably

    _____   periodicals

    _____   books

    _____   Internet

F.   You **must** have your GSW id with you to

    _____   check out books

    _____   ask a Reference librarian for assistance

    _____   use the library's public computers

G.   The library charges 10 cents per page to

    _____   print articles and web pages

    _____   print lists of books

ASSIGNMENT #1:
FOCUSING YOUR RESEARCH AND BROWSING THE COLLECTION

name	cpo box	lib res class time	R course

1.   Decide on a possible topic for your research and state it below.

2.   According to the Library of Congress classification handout, in which call number areas might you expect to find information on your topic? Provide more than one if applicable.

3.   Browse the reference collection to locate encyclopedias and dictionaries that will help you focus your topic. Browse by call number areas: AE for general encyclopedias and whatever call number areas you chose in question 2 for specialized encyclopedias.   Give the specific titles of one general and one specialized encyclopedia or dictionary that you consulted. **Do not use items from Oversize or the Index Area.**

GENERAL_____

SPECIALIZED_____

4.   What words, subject phrases, key terms, etc., will you use to research your topic? List a minimum of six (6).

InfoTrail

Library Assignment 1 - Choosing and Focusing Your Topic

NOTE: If you are completing InfoTrail as a class assignment, you must complete all the exercises. When you click the "submit" button at the bottom of the assignment, it will be emailed to your professor. If you wish you may also print out the assignment to hand in. It is a good idea to keep a copy for yourself.

Purpose:
To define an appropriately focused research topic and identify useful keywords for that topic.

Select your Instructor from the list: | Instructor Name ▼ |

Select your class from the list: | Class Name ▼ |

Your Name: |

Your Email: |

1. Choose a topic from the following list or use a topic of your own choosing if you have something definite in mind. At this point, you should be thinking of concepts or general topics, but if your topic is too broad, like "violence" for example, you should try to narrow it to a particular focus.
Choose one of the topics below or type in your own.

- ○ Women in the American West
- ○ Ethics of Violence
- ○ Religion and Culture

- ○ Technology in education
- ○ Teens and violence
- ○ Edgar Allen Poe

|_____| (fill in your topic)

2. List some subtopics or different aspects of this topic that you might investigate:

|_____ ▲ |
| |
|_____ ▼ |

3. Choose the subtopic listed above that you would like to research and type it in the box.

|_____|

4. What about this topic do you want to find out? Be specific. Type a question that expresses your research focus. For example: "What impact has technology had on education?" **This should not be a yes or no question, but an open-ended type of question.** If you are having trouble with this, see your instructor or the Reference Librarian for help.
Type your research question here.

5. Read the question you wrote in number two. Which key words from that question express the most relevant concepts in your question? Which keywords would probably be present in the title or subject of a source that answered your question? (In the case of my question, "technology", "impact", and "education" would all be likely to be present in a source that really answered my question.)
List the two or three key words from your question that are the most relevant to your topic.

6. Can you think of any alternative terms for your key words? (In my case, I might search under "computers" instead of "technology", or "effect" instead of "impact".
List your alternative key words here.

SUBMIT   CLEAR FORM

[http://library.uscolo.edu/infotrail/focus1.html]

Library Assignment 2 - Identifying Sources

NOTE: If you are completing InfoTrail as a class assignment, you must complete all the excercises. When you click the "submit" button at the bottom of the assignment, it will be emailed to your professor. If you wish you may also print out the assignment to hand in. It's a good idea to keep a copy for yourself just in case! You must complete Exercise 1 - Choosing Your Topic before you start Assignment 2.

Purpose:
To identify potential sources of information on your topic.

Select your Instructor from the list: | Instructor Name ▼ |

Select your class from the list: | Class Name ▼ |

Your Name: | |

Your Email: | |

1. Think about the research question you formed in Exercise 1 - Choosing Your Topic. Who or what organization do you think might have the information you need to answer your question? (For example, a government agency, a professor doing research, a private company, etc.)
In the blanks below, list several possible sources of information.

A. | |

B. | |

C. | |

2. In what format do you think this person/organization might make this information available to the public? (For example, published in a journal, on a Web site, in a book, through personal contact, etc.)
The blanks below correspond to those in number one.
In each blank, enter where you think you would find the information from the source you listed above.

A. [_____]

B. [_____]

C. [_____]

3. How could you access the information sources you listed in number two? Would these sources be available in a library database, in print, on the Internet, or some other way? (For example information published in a journal could be accessed in a library periodical index.)
The blanks below correspond to those in number two.
In each blank, enter where you think you would access the resources you listed above.

A. [_____]

B. [_____]

C. [_____]

[SUBMIT]   [CLEAR FORM]

[http://library.uscolo.edu/infotrail/identify.html]

Information & Technology
Research Assignment #2
EBSCOhost/Gale InfoTrac

Name_____

Class Day and Time_____

Research Topic_____

Part I: Using **EBSCOhost** locate a full-text article on your topic (use the same topic from Research Assignment #1). It should be at least 2 printed pages in length (10pts). Print and staple the article to the back of this form (10pts). Later you will use this article in your "Mock" Research Paper. You will be graded on how relevant the article is to your research topic (20pts).(hint: *Do not use* **any type of** *review for this assignment.*)

Database Used: (5pts)_____

Part II: Using **Gale InfoTrac** locate a full-text article on your topic (use the same topic from Research Assignment #1). It should be at least 2 printed pages in length (10pts). Print and staple the article to the back of this form (10pts). Later you will use this article in your "Mock" Research Paper. You will be graded on how relevant the article is to your research topic (20pts).(hint: *Do not use* **any type** *of review for this assignment.*)

Database Used: (5pts) _____

Now that you have completed your research please answer the following questions. Compare the research you did on the Internet with NC Live. Which resource was the most useful for your topic? Which resource enabled you to retrieve the most specific information? In the future when conducting research where do you intend to start? What problems did you have with the Internet? What problems did you have with NC Live?(10pts) **Be sure to give complete answers**.

_____
_____
_____
_____
_____
_____
_____

ASSIGNMENT #4
LOCATING RELEVANT PERIODICAL ARTICLES

_____   _____   _____   _____
       name   cpo box   lib res class time   R course

What is your research topic? _____

PART I: SUBJECT-SPECIFIC ONLINE RESOURCES

Of the specialized databases covered in class (MLA, ERIC, Omnifile's Social Science Index, PsycInfo and PsycArticles, ATLA Religion Index, Basic BIOSIS and BioOne, and IIMP), which would you use to gather relevant references on:

    a.   lesson plans for teaching about the Underground Railroad
    b.   themes of disguise in William Shakespeare
    c.   moral implications of the Sermon on the Mount
    d.   acquiring a second language
    e.   multiple personality disorder
    f.   the life cycle of the gypsy moth
    g.   analysis of Bach's Brandenberg Concertos
    h.   the history of the electoral college
    i.   your research topic listed above

PART II: OPTIONS FOR THE FULL TEXT OF ARTICLES

1. Using the database(s) you chose for your answer to Ii, find one journal citation relevant to your topic. **Attach a printout** of the citation. (You can get this by e-mailing the citation to yourself or copying and pasting it into a Word document).

2. Consult Serial Solutions to see if you can access your article ONLINE in full text. **If no**, print enough of the screen to show your unsuccessful title search. **If yes**, print the appropriate paragraph for your title search. (Again, you can do these by copying and pasting into a Word document.). _Circle_ all the databases that have your article. **Attach** the printout either way.

3. Now find out if Houghton College has this particular article in paper by searching our holdings in GRACE. **If no**, _print the screen_ which shows your unsuccessful title search. **If yes**, _print the screen_ which shows our holdings and _circle_ the volume number you need. Also _circle_ the location of the journal which contains the article you cited (whether BOUND, MICROFORM, CURRENT, etc.) **Attach** the printout either way.

Finding Articles Worksheet

Answer the following questions for each index.

1. Index name:

2. How far back in time does this index go? (Hint: Check the written or onscreen instructions, or look at the date on the earliest volume for print indexes.)

3. Term(s) you searched for:

4. Term(s) under which articles were listed:

5. Is it easy to find articles on your subject? What made it easy or difficult?

6. Write the titles of three of the periodicals that have articles on your topic, according to this index. For each periodical, indicate whether or not the Library owns the issue in which the article appears. If it does, give the call number.

Put your answer to this question on only one of the worksheets:

7. Which of the indexes do you like the best, and why?

Send comments and suggestions about this page to: Information Services
Last Updated: August 16, 2000

Library Home | Catalyst | Databases | Periodicals List | Research Guides | Site Search
The Library, Humboldt State University, One Harpst St., Arcata, California 95521-8299
Telephone: 707-826-3441   Fax: 707-826-3440

ASSIGNMENT #3
DIFFERENTIATING BETWEEN SCHOLARLY AND POPULAR PERIODICALS

_____ _____ _____ _____
        name   cpo box   lib res class time   R course

What is your research topic? _____
What style guide are you using?   ___MLA   ___APA   ___Turabian
                                   ___other (indicate which one_____)

1. Look for periodical articles on your topic using the **print indexes** discussed in class. Use **two different index titles** that you've deemed appropriate to your topic. Which indexes did you select?

      a..

      b.

2. Copy citations for 2 periodical articles (NOT book chapters or essays) out of the indexes, one from EACH of the index titles. Before you write your selections down, make sure that at least one of the articles is in a periodical issue that Houghton owns **in paper.**

      a.

      b.

3. Locate the appropriate issue of the Houghton-owned periodical. Take a look at the article and the journal as a whole.   Indicate whether the article is from a scholarly or popular periodical.

      _____scholarly   or   _____popular.

      WHY? (give at least 3 reasons based on evaluation criteria covered in class):

        a.

        b.

        c.

4. Provide a citation for this article IN APPROPRIATE BIBLIOGRAPHIC CITATION FORMAT using the style guide you selected above. (Remember that you will have to adjust the citation format based on whether you decided that the periodical was scholarly or popular.) Note page and paragraph numbers you consulted in the style guide:

      a.   style guide page/paragraph numbers:

      b.   citation

Information & Technology
Research Assignment #1
The World Wide Web

Instructions: Using one of the Internet search tools introduced in class (i.e. Yahoo, Google, Profusion, etc) find one web page or web document that is related to your topic. Print one page from the source and staple the sheet to the back of this form. Note: In order to grade this assignment you must turn in at least one printed page from the web source that you locate.

DO NOT PRINT a list of links. *Make sure that you print the web page or document that contains the information you intend to use in your mock research paper.*

You will be graded on the validity of your site and how relevant the site is to your research topic. This will count for 50% of your grade.

Name_____

Class Day / Time_____

Research Topic_____

Web Browser Used_____

Search Engine or Subject Directory Used_____

URL for the search engine or directory that you used:

_____

Answer the following questions about the web page you located:

1. URL for the web page you located (make sure it is complete):

    _____

2. Who is the author of the web page? _____
    (*hint: If you can not determine the author then you do not want to use the page or document for research purposes.*)

3. What is the title of the web page? _____

4. Give your date of access (the date you found the web page)_____

5. Based on the criteria for Evaluating Web Resources (handout) explain why this document is appropriate for your topic in five to eight sentences?

    _____
    _____
    _____
    _____
    _____

Name_____ Date_____ FS 100 Section_____

Web Search Service Exercise

1. Use *Alta Vista* and *Google* to search for information on Johann Sebastian Bach. Which of the two search engines found the Bach home page immediately?

2. Now link to a website that allows you to download MIDI files of his music. What is that site called?

3. *Ask Jeeves* for information on the Dash diet. What medical condition does that diet seek to aid? What other links does *Ask Jeeves* recommend?

4. Do a search in a search service of your choice using Boolean AND. Find information on the Crusades and Venice. In which Crusade are the Venetians especially important?

5. Find the text of *Ut Unum Sint*. When was that document issued? By whom? What is its topic? What search service did you use to find it?

6. Find a site on the web that displays the full text of Medieval source documents. What is the name of the site you found? What search service did you use? How many steps after contacting with the service did you need?

7. Use a search directory (not a search engine) to find the home page of the University of Pittsburgh and a picture of the Cathedral of Learning. How many hyperlink clicks did you need in order to find it?

8. Find a site on the web that illustrates binary arithmetic. Which search engine did you use? How many steps did you need to take before you found it?

9. Find an investment report on the AMD Corporation. Use *Northern Light*. If you are successful, write down the URL of the site that gives you the information. Then go to *EBSCOhost* and use *Business Source Premier*. How many steps were required for each search before you located the information?

10. Who was the pope who excommunicated Martin Luther? In what year did this happen? What service did you use to find this information? How many steps did it take?

DOCUMENTS : *Rubrics*

Bibliography Rating Scale

Criteria	Score
1. The appropriateness of the material cited as sources of information for a scholarly paper in biology. (Appropriateness = reputation of source, age of source, etc.)	5 4 3 2 1 0
2. The appropriateness of the material cited as sources of information for the particular subject being studied. (Appropriateness = reputation of source, age, author authority)	5 4 3 2 1 0
3. A reasonable number of primary sources, from a variety of titles. This shows some confrontation with the indexing services that are available. (1 point/source)	5 4 3 2 1 0
4. Inclusion of the several most important secondary sources and texts in the field being studied. (2 points/source)	5 4 3 2 1 0
5. Number of references. Anything less than 10 items would raise the questions of completeness. This will vary greatly from subject to subject and must be considered a minor point. (Less than 4 sources-0 pts.; 4-6 sources-1 pt.; 7-9 sources-2 pts.; 10 or more sources-3pts.)	3 2 1 0
6. Consistent acceptable format used in the cited literature section. (Inconsistent format, incomplete information-0 pts.; inconsistent format, complete information-1 pt.; unacceptable consistent format, complete information-2 pts.; acceptable, consistent format, complete information-3pts.)	3 2 1 0

Rubric for Assessing Research Papers

ACRL Information Literacy Competency Standard #1

*Variety of sources (1.2.c & d)	all from one source type	mix of 2 source types	mix of more than 2 source types	
Sources satisfy research/information need	severely unbalanced (most important literature is missing)	adequate (viewpoints limited but adequate)	balanced (good representation of viewpoints)	comprehensive

ACRL Information Literacy Competency Standard #3

Timeliness of sources (3.2.a)	inappropriate dates for topic	mix of appropriate and inappropriate	appropriate dates for all materials	
Authority/ Reliability of sources (3.2.a)	all inappropriate authorities	mix of authoritative and non-author.	all reliable authorities	

ACRL Information Literacy Competency Standard #4

Use of reference(s) to evaluate or illustrate specific points (4.1.c; 4.3; 3.1)	doesn't use references OR quotes or references don't seem to be serving any purpose–are just "stuck in"	quotes or references serve a purpose but are generally not well-used	uses references or quotes: -for background information -to support student's thesis -as support for a specific point	
Integrates quotes effectively (style: block quotes, signal phrases, etc.) (4.3; 3.1)	not integrated well	some quotes effectively integrated (some not)	most quotes effectively integrated	sophisticated use of quotes
Citing/ documenting materials in text (4.1.c)	many errors (did not cite accurately or neglected to cite source)	most are correct but minor errors are numerous	all entries conform to required style with few punctuation errors	

ACRL Information Literacy Competency Standard #5

Bibliography/works cited: *one style* (5.3.a)	many errors	most entries conform to style; minor errors are numerous	all entries conform to required style with few punctuation errors	
Bibliog/works cited: *complete* info. (5.3.a)	incomplete	most are complete; some missing info.	information is complete	
Are all sources cited in text listed on Works Cited page or bibliography? (5.3.a)	source list is incomplete	source list is complete		
Are all sources listed on Works Cited page cited in paper?	none	some	most	all
Evidence of plagiarism (uncredited sources) 5.3.a	throughout paper	some	none	

Overall Rating – Student Use of Outside Sources

Does this student know how to use outside sources, as evidenced in this paper?	poor use of sources	some ability shown	good use	sophisticated use

*All standards & references to performance indicators (numbers in left column of rubric) are tied to ACRL's *Information Literacy Competency Standards for Higher Education* (2000).
Variety of sources = books, journal articles, popular magazines, websites, etc.

Developed: Beth Mark & Lawrie Merz 4/27/01

Assessment of First Year Seminar Paper Sample
Selection, Use, and Citation of Sources – Report to Faculty, Fall 1999

SOURCE SELECTION				
Variety of source types (e.g., books, journal or magazine articles, etc.)	21=23.3% all from one type of source	41=45.5% mix of 2 types of sources	28=31% mix of more than 2 types of sources	
Timeliness of sources (for topic)	0 inappropriate dates	5=4.5% mix of appropriate and inappropriate	85=94.4% appropriate dates for all materials	
Authority/ Reliability of sources for topic	0 all inappropriate authorities	40=44.4% mix of authoritative and non-authoritative	50=55.5% all reliable authorities	
INFORMATION USE				
Sources satisfy research/ information need	10=11% severely unbalanced (most important literature is missing)	33=36.6% adequate (viewpoints limited but adequate)	37=41% balanced (good representation of viewpoints)	10=11% comprehensive
Use of reference(s) to evaluate or illustrate specific points	2=2.2% doesn't use references OR quotes or references don't seem to be serving any purpose–are just "stuck in"	18=20% quotes or references serve a purpose but are generally not well-used	36=40% (good)　34=37.7% (better)　uses references or quotes: -for background information -to support student's thesis -as support for a specific point	
Integrates quotes effectively (style: block quotes, signal phrases, etc.)	6=6.6% not integrated well	23=25.5% some quotes effectively integrated (some not)	35=38.8% most quotes effectively integrated	26=28.8% sophisticated use of quotes
CITATION				
Citing/ documenting materials *in text*	18=20% many errors (did not cite accurately or neglected to cite source)	21=23.3% most are correct but minor errors are numerous	51=56.6% all entries conform to required style with few punctuation errors	
Bibliography/works cited: *one style*	14=15.5% many errors	30=33.3% most entries conform to style; minor errors are numerous	46=51% all entries conform to required style with few punctuation errors	
Bibliog/works cited: *complete* information	4=4.4% incomplete	40=44.4% most are complete; some missing info.	46=51% information is complete	
Are all sources cited in text listed on Works Cited page or bibliography?	15=16.6% source list is incomplete	75=83.3% source list is complete		
Are all sources in Works Cited list cited in paper?	1=1.1% none	9=10% some	19=21% most	61=67.7% all
Evidence of plagiarism or uncredited sources	3=3.3% throughout paper	31=34.4% some	56= 62% none	
OVERALL RATING – STUDENT USE OF OUTSIDE SOURCES				
Overall rating: Does student know how to use outside sources, as evidenced in this paper?	2=2.2% poor use of sources	24=26.6% some ability shown	47=52% good use	17=18.8% sophisticated use

Developed by Beth Mark & Lawrie Merz 4/27/01

New Mexico State University

Research Project Reference Rating (RPRR) Bibliography Assessment Rubric

Description   Score (Circle)

Description			
1) Student provides **justification for selecting sources** or how they will be relevant to the project (annotated bibliography or paragraph in project; 1 = yes; 0 = no)		1	0
2) *MLA or APA Citation Style Format* (for the references)			
a) **Order** of entries (alphabetical by author or title if no author; 1 = yes; 0 = no)		1	0
b) **Spacing**, double or single (1 = correct; 0 = incorrect)		1	0
c) **Indentation** (1 = correct; 0 = incorrect)		1	0
d) **Punctuation** (1 = correct; 0 = incorrect)		1	0
e) **Capitalization** (1 = correct; 0 = incorrect)		1	0
f) **Spelling, Abbreviations** (1 = correct; 0 = incorrect)		1	0
g) **Italics/Underlining** (1 = correct; 0 = incorrect)		1	0
h) **Names** (1 = correct; 0 = incorrect)		1	0
i) **Dates** (1 = correct; 0 = incorrect)		1	0
j) **Volume, Issue, Number, Pagination** (1 = correct; 0 = incorrect)		1	0
k) **Uniform Resource Locators** (1 = correct; 0 = incorrect)		1	0
l) **Order within entries** (1 = correct; 0 = incorrect)		1	0
m) **Information** sufficient to locate source (2 = complete; 1 = some errors; 0 = inadequate)	2	1	0
3) *Source **Balance***			
a) Adequate **number** to cover topic (2 = 4 or more unique; 1 = 1 to 3)	2	1	0
b) Includes <u>key</u> **primary** sources (2 = 2 or more; 1 = at least one; 0 = none)	2	1	0
c) Includes <u>key</u> **secondary** sources (2 = 2 or more; 1 = at least one; 0 = none)	2	1	0
d) **Variety** (at least one from each of the following categories; count each cite once)			
i. Background (encyclopedia, dictionary, yearbook, reference)		1	0
ii. Book		1	0
iii. Government document or .gov web site		1	0
iv. Scholarly journal article		1	0
v. Popular or magazine article		1	0
vi. Newspaper, wire service, radio, TV, or web cast article		1	0
vii. Web site		1	0
viii. Interview, speech, lecture, or other primary source		1	0
ix. Other appropriate source		1	0
4) **Quality** of Sources for the Selected Topic			
a) **Currency** (rapidly changing fields require recent materials; historical topics require a broad spectrum; 0 = older or inappropriate sources; dates not provided; 1 = a mix of older and recent sources; 2 = all within the last 10 years or appropriate to the topic)	2	1	0
b) **Authority** of author and sponsor (produced by a government agency, higher education institution, or other reputable organization with expertise on the topic; 0 = all inappropriate authorities; 1 = a mix of authoritative and non-authoritative; 2 = all reasonable authorities)	2	1	0
c) **Objectivity** and **Accuracy** (0=all biased, inaccurate, or commercial sources; 1=a mix of objective and biased sources; 2=all objective sources projecting a factual, informational approach)	2	1	0
5) *Coverage, Scope, and Depth of Sources Cited*			
a) Relevant to the General **Field**	2	1	0
b) Relevant to the Specific **Topic** (the right sources to obtain information on this topic)	2	1	0
c) **Appropriate** for an academic paper (include audience; overall assessment)	2	1	0
TOTAL SCORE			

Key to Terms used in the RPRR

Accuracy	Fact and truth based content.
Appropriate	The extent to which the bibliography provides an adequate set of resources for an academic paper on this topic
Audience	Materials must be appropriate to a college-educated or academic audience; materials designed for K-12 students are not acceptable
Authority	Materials sponsored, produced, or written by government agencies, higher education institutions, or other reputable organizations with expertise on the topic are appropriate for an academic paper. Materials written by a scholar in the field are also appropriate.
Currency	Materials should be as current as possible. In general, sources written within the last 10 years are acceptable. Historical topics require primary materials contemporary with the event and recent materials to analyze the impact of the event on current society. Technology, government, legal, and many social issues require very recent materials.
Format	Follow the Citation Style Format recommended by the department or library as required by the instructor of the course.
Information	If there is sufficient information to allow you to obtain all the sources, assign a "2."
Number	Scorers may apply broad discretion in determining whether the number of citations is adequate to cover the topic. Four citations is the minimum to cover a topic, but is not necessarily adequate. Some students list many pages on a single web server—these all count as a single citation.
Objectivity	Sources written to present a factual approach to a topic are objective as opposed to sources written from a particular point of view. If students include materials written with a bias, they should include sources presenting opposing viewpoints as well. Information taken from websites primarily designed to sell a product (.com domain) have especially dubious objectivity. Information taken from .org domain websites may come from non-profits or organizations with a particular bias. Materials found on .edu domain web sites may not be sponsored or approved by the school.
Order	The order of the entries should be alphabetical by the author's last name, sponsoring organization, or title. Do not count off for numbering of citations.
Primary	Original material, the firsthand observations of someone present at an event, speech, interview, letter, memoir, autobiography, legislation, etc.
Secondary	Modified, analyzed, framed according to a particular perspective, a journalistic or textbook presentation of facts or an event
Variety	Student bibliographies should include information sources from the broadest possible range of types. Count each citation only once; if a citation falls into two or more categories, assign it to a category not yet used; do not count the citation if other citations took up to the appropriate categories.
GENERAL	
	Double-space in both APA and MLA; MLA underlines titles; APA italicizes titles
	Be fairly strict in Section 2); use judgment in Section 5)
	It is not necessary to circle all the 0 scores. It helps in Section 2) to ensure you examine the bibliography for each criteria
	If the bibliography does not include a journal article or website, the bibliography receives a 0 in 2) j or k.

[Developer/Contact: Anne C. Moore (annem@library.umass.edu)]

University of Charleston

Rating Scale
SSCI 221

and Social Sciences Majors

Student Name:

Evaluator:

Date:

A hypothetical research topic will be assigned to the student with instructions to devise and demonstrate a successful search strategy. Topics will be selected by the Instruction Librarian from *10,000 Ideas for Term Papers, Projects and Reports, 3rd ed.* by Kathryn Lamm [R 808.02 L188te3 1991] located in the Reference Room. The student will:

(Evaluator will circle most appropriate rating for activity)

1. Ascertain the subject field of the topic and the discipline into which the subject field fits.

> 3. The subject field and the discipline are ascertained
> 2. Either subject field or the discipline is ascertained
> 1. Neither subject field nor the discipline are ascertained

2. Determine appropriate Subject Heading/Term(s) that best describe the concept(s) of the topic.

> 3. Library of Congress Subject Heading/Term(s) descriptive of the concept(s) are used
> 2. Invalid Keyword(s) -- non-Subject Headings -- somewhat descriptive of the concepts are used
> 1. Invalid, nondescriptive Subject Headings or Keywords are used

3. Select appropriate/discipline-specific access tool.

> 3. Selects catalog and discipline-specific electronic (or print) index
> 2. Selects only a general index or only the catalog
> 1. Selects neither a discipline-specific index nor catalog

4. [Obtains] one factual, objective source within the Library's collection.

> 3. Obtains a factual, objective source within the Library's collection
> 2. Obtains a factual source outside the Library's collection (Website outside library vendors)
> 1. Obtains a nonfactual, subjective source within or outside the Library's collection

5. [Obtains] two recent analytical sources (either on-site or Web-based vendor).
Source 1:

> 3. Obtains recent analytical source (either on-site or Web-based vendor)
> 2. Obtains non-analytical source
> 1. Obtains no source relevant to the topic

6. [Obtains] two recent analytical sources (either on-site or Web-based vendor).
Source 2:

> 3. Obtains recent analytical source (either on-site or Web-based vendor)
> 2. Obtains non-analytical source
> 1. Obtains no source relevant to the topic

7. Explains briefly how the two analytical sources relate to the topic and to each other.

> 3. Explains briefly how the two analytical sources relate to the topic and to each other
> 2. Explains how two (or one) analytical source(s) relate either to the topic or to each other
> 1. Cannot explain how any acquired source relates to the topic or to each other

8. Selects appropriate access tool to obtain one relevant Website.

> 3. Selects appropriate access tool to obtain one relevant Website
> 2. Selects appropriate access tool but fails to obtain relevant Website
> 1. Selects inappropriate access tool and fails to obtain relevant Website

9. Evaluates acquired sources according to evaluation criteria of accuracy, authority, currency

> 3. Successfully evaluates acquired sources according to all evaluation criteria
> 2. Partially evaluates all (or only some) acquired sources
> 1. Cannot evaluate acquired sources according to any criteria

10. Demonstrates knowledge of proper citation format for discipline and type of resource

> 3. Successfully employs proper citation format for sources acquired
> 2. Employs proper citation format for some (or all) sources with aid of style manual
> 1. Cannot cite sources in proper format and does not seek assistance in style manual

---

Numeric Summation: _____

26 - 30 Student demonstrates competency in the academic library research process.

20 - 25 Student has grasp of overall concepts and is familiar with the research process, but would benefit from further practice with strategy formation and resource familiarization.

15 - 19 Student has inadequate familiarity with the research process and library resources; cannot proceed with demonstration without prompting. Re-orientation to resources and one-on-one practice sessions are indicated.

10 - 14 Student demonstrates no familiarity with the research process and little, if any, familiarization with the library's resources. Course should be repeated or an Individual Learning Plan should be developed in collaboration with the student's academic advisor.

Descriptive Summation and Comments:

Source consulted: *Classroom Assessment*. Airasian, Peter W. New York:McGraw-Hill, 1991. See Chapter 7: "Performance Assessment".

[Developer/Contact: Susan M. Foster-Harper (sfoster@ucwv.edu)]   8/30/2000

[http://www.uchaswv.edu/library/instruct/rating.html]

DOCUMENTS : *Tests*

LIBRARY RESEARCH FINAL PROJECT

Your final project is to create a library "pathfinder" on a topic relevant to your R course–ideally, the topic you have already research or will soon research for a paper or speech in that class. **The deadline will be two weeks from the date you receive these guidelines, at a time designated by your instructor.**

Please choose the style manual you will follow throughout, and note it in your heading.

What is a library "pathfinder"? You now have lots of expertise navigating the library for your particular topic, so you'll be writing up a brief report that passes on that expertise to someone else who might have to research the same topic in the Houghton library in the future.

Your pathfinder should have four sections:

A. BROWSING THE REFERENCE COLLECTION
B. SEARCHING G.R.A.C.E. FOR MONOGRAPHS (BOOKS)
C. PERIODICAL INDEXES (PAPER AND ONLINE)
D. WORLD WIDE WEB SITES

For each section you will want to provide:

1. a short introduction, which may include advice on where materials are located in the library; on search terms, commands, or strategies one might use; on selecting an appropriate index, etc.

2. at least two (2) items that might prove helpful in researching that topic, properly cited according to the style manual you chose above. In Sections A and B, be sure to add the Houghton Library call number for each resource. In Section C, mention some appropriate periodicals indexes *plus* **at least two** relevant articles found in those indexes.

3. an annotation (brief summary) of the special features and content of each of the sources.

A sample annotation might look something like this:

Magill, F.N., ed. *Magill's Literary Annual.* Englewood Cliffs, NJ: Salem Press, 1977-present. **REF PN 44 .M282**
Issued annually in two volumes, this set provides plot summaries and critical assessment of outstanding novels, plays, and collections of poetry and short stories published during each year beginning in 1976. The second volume of each year has an author index for all previous volumes.

NAME:_____

GS113   Exam   4/24/01

Log on to Expanded Academic ASAP for questions 1 and 2.

1. Perform a keyword phrase search for articles about the **Electoral College.**

    a. How many articles did you retrieve?

    b. How many of them are in referenced journals?

    c. How many of the 1st 20 refereed articles are NOT available in full text online, BUT are available in print or microform in the library?

    d. Of all the refereed articles, how many are available in full text online?

2. One of your professors gives you a bibliography of journal articles with the instructions to find one of the articles and write a summary of it. You select the following journal article:

    Voeks, Robert. "African medicine and magic in the Americas."
    The Geographical Review 83 no. 1 (1993):66-78.

When you look up the journal title in LION, it tells you it is only available in full text through Expanded Academic ASAP. Find the full text of the article and write down one of the subject headings that was assigned to this article that has no more than 3 related articles (other than the name of the journal).

Click on the link to the other article and mark the **first 3 articles.** E-mail me your marked list (citations only). henderson_e@mail.lynchburg.edu PUT YOUR FIRST NAME IN THE SUBJECT FIELD.

3. Log on to Infomine < infomine.ucr.edu> and find a website related to the topic of the Voeks article for Question 2. The subject headings used by Expanded Academic ASAP are not the same as the subject headings used by Infomine, so you may have the think of alternative synonyms. You do not have to used the same heading that you used for the marked list.

    a. Area of Infomine you searched_____

    b. Subject heading or keyword searched_____

    c. Title of Web site and URL_____

4. a. Which kind of Internet search tool would you expect to return more "hits"? Circle your answer.
        1. subject directory
        2. search engine?

b. Which would you expect to retrieve a higher percentage of relevant sites?
   1. subject directory
   2. search engine
c. Explain the main difference(s) between the two search tools in no more than a couple of sentences.

5. When you run a search for **rap music** (search A.) in one of the search engines, it retrieves over 864,101 sites. When you search for **rap and music**, (search B) only 81, 336 sites are retrieved. What can you surmise from this about how this search engine searches multiple terms? (Details please! How will the words appear in the retrieved articles?)

Search A?

Search B?

What would you type to be sure that the words **rap music** appear in all retrieved items in that specific order?

6. Write a Boolean search sentence to retrieve articles for a paper on the topic **"Antibacterial cleaning products encourage the development of antibiotic resistant strains of bacteria."** Be succinct, i.e., don't use unnecessary words! Do include obvious synonyms.

7. a. If looking for a web page from the University of Iowa, what top level domain name would you   expect to be in the main domain name part of the URL?

b. For a web page put out by the State Department?

c. For a web page put out by Stars?

8. Write a defense or refute the following statement:

"If it was really wrong to cut and paste sections of papers found online into a term paper, it wouldn't be so easy."

Manhattanville College

Annotated Bibliography

The final project for this course will consist of *an annotated bibliography of at least 10 information sources*, all of which relate to a narrowly defined topic of your choice.

Begin with an introduction explaining the scope of your topic, so that the reader will understand the focus of your research. The introduction may be two or three paragraphs long. Then list the items alphabetically by author, using MLA style bibliographic format. Each item must be followed by an annotation, or descriptive *and* critical evaluation, demonstrating clearly how this item relates to your topic.

The purpose of the final project is for each student to demonstrate an understanding of the research skills taught in this course, therefore, you should include a variety of information sources in your bibliography. It is suggested that you include the following types of sources: 1 book, 2 scholarly journals, 3 reputable magazines, 1 newspaper and 3 other sources of your choice. You may also include audiovisual materials, government documents, internet documents or personal interviews.

The final project must be typed. Projects are due one week after the last class. Grades will be lowered for papers submitted after the due date. Along with the final project, you must hand in photocopies of:
title page and verso of each book included
First page of each periodical article included (if you retrieve the article online, you must hand in a print out of the first page)

Before Handing in your Final Project!
...ask yourself the following questions

1. Have I included an introduction of at least two paragraphs which explains the topic I have chosen and the special focus I have brought to the topic?
2. Do the items I have chosen pertain to the topic as I have described it in the introduction?
3. Have I followed correctly, the MLA style of bibliographic format for books and periodical articles?
4. Are my annotations written using correct grammar and spelling?
5. Have I followed the guidelines for writing annotations, providing critical evaluations of each source and not just simple abstracts?
6. Where possible, have I verified the credibility of the sources that I have chosen to include?
7. Is my final project neatly typed and does it present a pleasing appearance?
8. Have I provided photocopies of each title page and verso (for books) and of the first page of each periodical article included in my bibliography?

This page last updated on 08/08/01 06:41 PM
Please send comments & suggestions to library@mville.edu

[http://www.mville.edu/library/lis1001/finalproject.htm]

First Year Seminar Library Test

Instructions: You may take this test on-line only once. It is a timed test. You have 30 minutes to complete this assessment. The elapsed time appears at the bottom of your browser. A **1minute** warning will be displayed. If you have technical difficulties or need to retake the test to achieve a passing score, contact your liaison librarian.

Question 1 **What are keywords?**
❑ Subject headings chosen by librarians
❑ Significant words that you want to search
❑ Words that you search to find all books by a particular author

Question 2 **Publications such as magazines, journals, and newspapers are called:**
❑ Newsstands
❑ Periodicals
❑ Scholarly publications
❑ Spreadsheets

Question 3 **What is a periodical index?**
❑ The table of contents page of a specific journal
❑ A list of subjects, titles, etc., that locates articles in magazines or journals
❑ A database that only contains the full text of magazine articles

Question 4 **What is an abstract?**
❑ A summary of an article
❑ Bibliographic information (author, title, journal title, etc.)
❑ A quote from an article

Question 5 **What is a citation?**
❑ A summary of an article
❑ Bibliographic information (author, title, journal title, etc.)
❑ An illustration (chart, graph, etc.) from an article

Question 6 **What is the *best* type of material for finding information on a topic?**
❑ Books
❑ Magazines
❑ Magazines and journals
❑ Web sites
❑ It depends on the topic

Question 7   **If you want to find current information on computer viruses, which of these informational fields give you reason not to pursue this source?**
❑ AUTHOR: Fites, Philip.
❑ TITLE: Computer virus crisis.
❑ IMPRINT: New York: Harper, 1980.
❑ SUBJECT: Computer viruses.

Question 8   **Books and most other items in Messiah's library are classified by the Library of Congress (LC) call number system. The LC system places books on the shelf:**
❑ Alphabetically by author
❑ Next to other books about the same or a related subject
❑ Alphabetically by title
❑ In random order

Question 9   **Listed below in correct order are three book call numbers.**

(1)	(2)	(3)
D	D	D
65	1120	1143
.L72	.S87	.D38

Where would a book with the call number D1143 .M57 be placed in relation to the call numbers above?

❑ Before 1
❑ Between 1 and 2
❑ Between 2 and 3
❑ After 3

Question 10   **Listed below in correct order are three book call numbers.**

(1)	(2)	(3)
D	D	D
65	1120	1143
.L72	.S87	.D38

❑ Before 1
❑ Between 1 and 2
❑ Between 2 and 3
❑ After 3

Question 11

Periodicals in libraries can be arranged in a variety of ways. In Messiah's library they are shelved:
- ❑ By call number
- ❑ Alphabetically by title of periodical
- ❑ By subject covered
- ❑ By level of content: scholarly or popular

Question 12

The Library Catalog includes:
- ❑ Only books
- ❑ Books, videos, compact discs
- ❑ Journal articles and books
- ❑ Journal articles and newspaper articles

Question 13

When researching the topic *sexual harassment of women in the workplace*, which periodical index would probably NOT have much information appropriate to the topic?
- ❑ Social Sciences Abstracts
- ❑ Business Abstracts
- ❑ Art Abstracts
- ❑ Index to Legal Periodicals
- ❑ PsycFIRST (Psychological Abstracts)

Question 14

When performing a keyword search, the computer:
- ❑ Locates only titles that begin with the keyword
- ❑ Locates items that have the keyword anywhere in the title, subject headings, etc.
- ❑ Locates items alphabetically by subject

Question 15

You need to do research on the topic *drug problems among athletes*. Your first step is to identify some keywords. Which of the following is NOT a good key term to get useful results?
- ❑ Drug(s)
- ❑ Athlete(s)
- ❑ Steroid(s)
- ❑ Sport(s)
- ❑ Problem(s)

Question 16

Once you've done a keyword search and found at least one good book on your topic in a library catalog, which of the following would be the *best* strategy for finding others?
- ❑ Perform a title keyword search using the same key words
- ❑ Perform a subject search using one of the subject headings found on the record for the book
- ❑ Perform an author search

Question 17 **What can the Boolean operator AND allow you to do?**
❑ Expand your search results, retrieving a larger number of results
❑ Focus your search results, retrieving a smaller number of results

Question 18 **What can the Boolean operator OR allow you to do?**
❑ Expand your search results, retrieving a larger number of results
❑ Focus your search results, retrieving a smaller number of results

Question 19 **What would you find if you searched for *television AND newspapers*?**
❑ Records containing *both* words (television, newspapers)
❑ Records containing *either* or *both* words (television, newspapers)

Question 20 **What *could* you get if you did the search: *Guatemala OR Mexico OR Honduras*?**
❑ Items that have all 3 words: Guatemala, Mexico, Honduras
❑ Items that have 2 out of the 3 words
❑ Items that have any one of the words: Guatemala, Mexico, Honduras
❑ All of the above answers

Question 21 **What would you get if you did the search: *girls AND esteem AND education*?**
❑ Items that have all 3 words: girls, esteem, education
❑ Items that have 2 out of the 3 words
❑ Items that have any one of the words: girls, esteem, education
❑ All of the above answers

Question 22 **If you search a database for *sports and women* and find too little information, which statement would help you *increase your results*?**
❑ Sports AND women AND female
❑ Sports AND (women OR female)
❑ Sports AND female
❑ Sports AND female OR women

Question 23 **What is the *VOLUME number* of the journal in this citation?**

Author: Scott, Ann.
Title: 'You Know People Talk': College Romance and Gossip.
Source: Midwestern Folklore 23(3): 27-35.
❑ 27
❑ 23
❑ 35
❑ 3

Question 24   **What is the *ARTICLE title* in this citation?**
A 'market correction' spurs news media's house cleaning
Advertising Age; Chicago; Sep 14, 1998; Randall Rothenberg
Volume: 69
Issue: 37
Start page: 34
❑ Advertising Age
❑ Randall Rothenberg
❑ A 'market correction' spurs news media's house cleaning

Question 25   **What is the *JOURNAL title* in this citation?**

The Memory Cure
Better Nutrition; Atlanta: Oct 1998; Patricia Andersen-Parrado
❑ The Memory Cure
❑ Better Nutrition
❑ Atlanta

Sample Quiz Questions

The following are actual questions taken from the OASIS quizzes. These questions are designed to give you an example of the types of questions that will appear on the quizzes for each chapter.

Chapter One - Defining the Research Topic and Determining the Information Requirements

1. Your assignment is:

Write a paper examining some of the major legal, ethical and/or social issues concerned with pornography on the Internet.

Which one set of search terms below will **best** help you find materials for your assignment?

___ legal, Internet, censorship
___pornography, children, Internet
___Internet, pornography, issues
___ethical, legal, Internet

2. Your assignment is to write a paper about the different styles of oil painting used by artists in the 1700's but you've discovered that there is far too much material than could be covered in a five page paper. Which one of the following lists of search terms below, best **narrows** your topic by being the most specific, thereby reducing your search results?

___ art, Europe, 1700's, styles
___ painting, styles, history
___oil painting, styles, 1700's, Italy

Chapter Two - Locating and Retrieving Relevant Information

1. Click <u>here</u> to open a window with InvestiGator, the Library's Online Catalog.

Do an *Author* search and determine which one of the books below was written by Terry McMillan. (close the window after your search)

___White Oleander
___Divine Secrets of the Ya-Ya Sisterhood
___Jazz
___How Stella Got Her Groove Back

2. Which **type** of reference source is shown in the table below?

___subject dictionary
___directory
___almanac
___yearbook

---

pixel - Contraction of picture element. The smallest element (a picture element) that a device can display and out of which the displayed image is constructed. See bit-mapped graphic.

PKCS - Acronym for Public Key Cryptography System. A set of standards, developed by RSA Data Security, that define an infrastructure for encrypted data - exchange on the Internet.

Plain Old Telephone Service - See POTS.

plain text document - A document that contains nothing by standard ASCII text, number, and punctuation characters.

planar board - See motherboard.

planar clock speed - The clock speed at which the motherboard operates. This speed may differ from the clock speed of the microprocessor, which may be two or more times faster.

plan file - A file in a UNIX user's home directory that was originally intended to display a colleague's schedule and work plans for the future when accessed with the finger utility. It is more often used for compiling humorous quotations or other informal uses.

plasma display - A display technology used with high-end laptop computers. The display is produced by energizing ionized gas held between two transparent panels. Synonymous with gas plasma display.

platen - In dot-matrix and letter-quality impact printers, the cylinder that guides paper through the printer and provides a backing surface for the paper when

---

Chapter Three - Using Databases for Accessing Information

1. Shown below is an article citation from the electronic database **ABI Inform** which covers the fields of business and management.

Title: "Mapping out your firm's success"
Source: *Black Enterprise*; New York; Mar 2000
Author: Mark Richard Moss; Volume 30; Issue 8; pp. 104-112
Subject Terms: Entrepreneurs, Strategic planning, Corporate objectives, Guidelines, Minority owned businesses.

Question: Would this article be included in the results of a Subject search for the phrase *strategic planning*?

___Yes
___No

2. Choose the **best** answer that completes the following statement.

By using the technique of *truncation* in a database search, you would:

___narrow your search to include less information
___limit your search to include less information
___use the terms *and, or, & not*
___broaden your search to include more information

Chapter Four - Using the World Wide Web for Accessing Information

1. All Web sites pages are routinely checked for the accuracy of the information presented on the page by the Internet Registry Service.

___True
___False

2. When a Web search tool such as, *AltaVista* uses *free-text indexing*, this means that the search tool will:

___allow you to search for free
___look for the term "free text" anywhere on the page retrieved by your search
___provide free links to other Web services
___look anywhere on the Web page for the search words that were entered

Chapter Five - Evaluating, Organizing, and Synthesizing Information

1. You are writing a paper for a history class on the ways in which the Spanish-American War impacted Amercan culture. You would like to use the information from a particular book, shown below.

Would the information found in the book be considered a primary source for your assignment?

___Yes
___No

The Rough Riders

Theodore Roosevelt

An immediate bestseller upon its release in 1899, *The Rough Riders* is Roosevelt's personal writings on his adventures in the Spanish-American War. A truly American crew of cowboys, scholars, land speculators, Native Americans and African Americans, the Rough Riders' triumphs and defeats are chronicled with riveting and engrossing detail.

From: The Rough Riders. New York: Bartleby.com, 1999

2. You are writing a paper about the migration of Africanized honey bees to the United States and you have found the following article:

"Flight of the Killer Bees." *Newsweek*, Nov. 14, 1994.Vol 117, No.19, p.25

Would this be considered a *scholarly journal article*?

___Yes
___No

Chapter Six - Communicating Using Information Technologies

1. If you want to send an electronic version of your paper to your professor and you are unsure of his/her computer skills, it would be best to:

___send the paper via E-mail as an attached file
___send the professor the address of your Web page
___send it in the body of a regular E-mail message
___send it as a Powerpoint presentation with graphics

2. You receive an E-mail message that begins with this header:

```
Date: Sat, 5 Jun 1999 14:41:04 -0700 (PDT)
From: Richard Smith rsmith@gotmail.com
To: computerwhiz@lab.berkeley.edu
Subject: Anthropology project
```

What is the username of the sender?

___Richard Smith
___computerwhiz
___lab.berkeley.edu
___rsmith

Chapter Seven - Legal and Ethical Information Issues

1. You are creating a Web page for a class assignment. According to the Fair Use section of U.S. Copyright law, you have the right to scan a picture from a book and use the image on your Web site without obtaining permission because your Web page will be used for non-profit educational purposes.

___True
___False

2. Choose the **best** answer for the following question.

*What is meant by the term **cookies** when used in connection with Web browsing software programs?*

___Cookies keep track of all material you have downloaded or printed to ensure that those items are in the public domain.
___Cookies register all the freeware you've downloaded to your computer.
___Cookies provide information to a Web server, such as your password or the options you selected the last time you visited a Web site.
___Along with cakes, cookies provide public domain software to those who register their computers.

Chapter Eight - Media Literacy

1. Choose the **best** answer that completes the following statement.

A person that is *media literate* can:

____ easily use all types of computer hardware and software and other forms of new technology

____use and find information of all types in a university library, including computer sources, microfilm, and indexes/abstracts

____read, analyze and critically evaluate information presented in a variety of formats (television, print, radio, computers, etc.)

____critically evaluate television programs and tell when they are trying to be persuaded

2. Choose the **best** answer for the following question.

When media try to identify a certain group of people to get their message across to, this group of people is known as a(n):

____narrowcasting audience
____demographic response
____audience poll
____target audience

[http://oasis.sfsu.edu/chapters/testsample.html]

Student data:

Please complete the following about yourself: SSN:_____

1. Class: (**Circle one number**)   Freshman....1   Sophomore....2   Junior....3   Senior....4

2. Age: _____

3. Gender: Female....1   Male....2

4. Please indicate your major at Shepherd. If you have not declared a major, write "Undeclared." If you have two majors, name both.

_____   _____

Questions:

1. Which of the following topics can reasonably be covered in a 5-page research paper?

(**Circle one number**)

Global air pollution...1
Global air pollution from fossil fuels...2
Fossil fuel use in the United States..3
Coal production in West Virginia..4
History of mining in Marshal County, WV...5

2. The best way to identify current and authoritative information for a research paper on coal as a national energy source is:

(**Circle one number**)

search the World Wide Web...1
check an encyclopedia..2
consult a book..3
use a periodical index...4
Don't know..5

3. What information can be discerned from this call number?   **TP325 .W82 1980**

(**Circle all that apply.**)

subject..1
author..2
title...3
where the book is located...4
the date of publication...5

4. If you were writing a paper on employment in the coal industry and you found a newspaper article with statistics indicating that there was a 10% decline in 1998, which of the following is the next best step?

(Circle one.)

Verify the accuracy of the figure by comparing with last year's newspaper...................1
Check the statistics in a government source...2
Use the data, being sure to cite the article in your paper...3
Just use the data...4
Check the data using a book about coal published in 1998..5

5. If your keyword search in the Library's online catalog on "public health United States" retrieves 827 records, what would be the best next step?

(Circle one.)

Add terms to the search and try again..1
Try searching under "United States public health"...2
Try the search again with fewer terms..3
Scan the list to choose the most relevant books...4
Find another topic..5

6. Suppose your perform a subject search in the library online catalog on the "French Revolution" and the computer retrieves zero results. Which one of the following best applies?

(Circle one.)

The library has no books on the subject...1
Adding more terms to the search will retrieve books on the topic...............................2
The library's books on the topic are listed under different terms.................................3
The system is down..4
Don't know..5

7. In an online database (i.e. Ebscohost) which search below would retrieve the greatest number of records?

(Circle one.)

cognition and emotion...1
cognition or emotion...2
cognition not emotion...3
emotional cognition..4
cognitive emotions...5

8. Decide whether each citation below (left column) refers to a book, a journal article, a World Wide Web site, or a government document.

(Circle one number for each citation.)

Citations. ✂	Book	Journal article	WWW site	Gov't document	Don't know
a) Oaklander, C.I. 1992. Pioneers in folk art collecting. Folk Art 17:48-55.	1	2	3	4	5
b) Birks, L.S. Electron probe microanalysis. Wiley-Interscience, 1972.	1	2	3	4	5
c) New Zealand. Dept. of Statistic. External trade: imports. 1973-74. Aug. 1977	1	2	3	4	5
e) University of Chicago Library. Slavic and East European Studies. http://www.lib.uchicago.edu/LibInfo/SourcesBy Subject/Slavic/	1	2	3	4	5

9. For your history class you must select a primary source and write a brief paper placing it in context. From the list below, choose the **one** best primary source on which to base your paper.

(Circle one.)

Chapter in your text book...1
Journal article..2
Scholarly monograph...3
Collection of letters...4
Critical biography..5

10. Identify the components of this Web site which help you evaluate the authority and accuracy of the information it provides.

(Circle all that apply.)

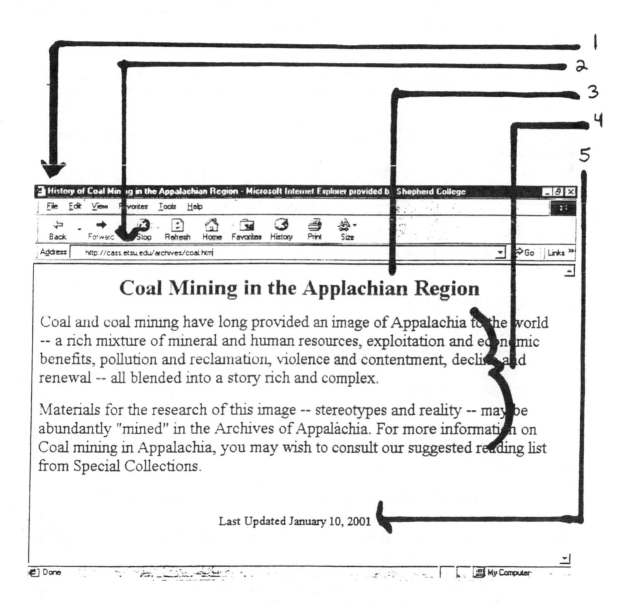

Library Research 102

Sample Exam Questions:
Library Research 102

The final examination for Library Research 102 consists of 50 multiple-choice questions based on information in the text, Making Sense of Library Research: A Guide for Undergraduate Students.

This practice test has 33 questions similar to those on the final exam. If you do not understand any question or an answer baffles you, please ask your instructor or any Reference Librarian for an explanation.

In addition to going over these sample questions, do the exercises at the end of each chapter in your text book.

Select the best response for each question:

1. The library service that allows professors to restrict the use of certain materials to short loan periods or in-library use is:

   ○ a. Interlibrary Loan service.
   ○ b. Reference Service.
   ○ c. Reserve Service.
   ○ d. Special Collections.
   ○ e. ABC Express service.

2. A library research strategy is a:

   ○ a. manual describing the proper format for a research paper.
   ○ b. handout available at the Reference Desk explaining how to get books from other libraries.
   ○ c. list of books on specific topics.
   ○ d. plan of action that gives direction to your research.
   ○ e. guidebook available for freshmen that provides a map of the library.

3. The main purpose of the Library of Congress classification system is to:

   ○ a. allow books to be shelved by height.
   ○ b. put every book by the same author in the same place.
   ○ c. arrange books alphabetically by their titles.
   ○ d. organize materials by subject, thus facilitating browsing.
   ○ e. keep books together according to publication date, so it is easy to find the most recent publications.

4. Which of the following statements about subject headings is not true?

    ○ a. There are books of subject headings that provide lists of topics under which you can find books in the library catalog.
    ○ b. Generally, personal and geographical names are not listed in the Library of Congress Subject Headings but are used in the Ramsey Library catalog.
    ○ c. Ramsey Library owns books for every valid subject heading listed in the Library of Congress Subject Headings.
    ○ d. The subject headings used in the Ramsey Library catalog come from the Library of Congress Subject Headings.
    ○ e. A subject heading is a word or phrase used to describe the subject content of a work.

5. You are looking for a book called Past and Present in Zimbabwe, but you cannot remember how to spell the last word in the title. Which of the following would be your best Title Search in the library catalog to be sure of finding this book?

    ○ a. pas,pre,Zim
    ○ b. past and present ??
    ○ c. past present in Z?e
    ○ d. past and present in Z
    ○ e. Zim?, past and present

6. You need to find books about the author Ellen Glasgow. What would be the best search to do on the library catalog?

    ○ a. Subject search for English literature
    ○ b. an Author search for Ellen Glasgow
    ○ c. a Title search for each work by Ellen Glasgow
    ○ d. a Subject search for Ellen Glasgow expressed as Glasgow, Ellen
    ○ e. a Keyword search for Glasgow

7. The Western North Carolina Library Network (WNCLN) is a network of colleges and universities that allows for the sharing of books and other library resources. The members of this network are:

    ○ a. UNCA, Mars Hill College, and A-B Tech.
    ○ b. Appalachian State University, Western Carolina University, and UNCA.
    ○ c. Montreat-Anderson College, UNCA, and Western Carolina University.
    ○ d. Mars Hill College, Warren Wilson College, and Montreat Anderson College.
    ○ e. UNC-Chapel Hill, UNC-Charlotte, and UNCA.

8. An encyclopedia:

    ○ a. is able to give you all possible information on any subject you may be researching.
    ○ b. is useful for getting background information on a topic.
    ○ c. is of absolutely no use as a starting point for research.
    ○ d. should be consulted only after you have looked at all other sources of information.
    ○ e. never includes bibliographies.

9. A dictionary that defines the terms and concepts of a particular discipline is:

○ a. a subject dictionary.
○ b. a slang dictionary.
○ c. a reverse dictionary.
○ d. an unabridged dictionary.
○ e. a polyglot dictionary.

10. The World Wide Web site with the address: http://www.earthwatch.org most likely belongs to a:

○ a. government agency.
○ b. commercial or for-profit business.
○ c. non-profit organization.
○ d. educational institution.
○ e. publisher in Oregon.

11. The type of Web search tool that organizes Web pages by category, usually in a hierarchy from broad subjects to narrow sub-catagories, is called a:

○ a. search engine.
○ b. meta-search engine.
○ c. directory.
○ d. Netseek.
○ e. Infolink.

12. You want to find every line in Byron's poetry where he used the word "mountain". You need to consult:

○ a. InfoTrac.
○ b. an atlas.
○ c. a reverse dictionary.
○ d. a periodical index.
○ e. a concordance.

13. You need to find some Web sites on freshwater fishing, excluding those dealing wth catfish. Which of the following searches in the Web search engine AltaVista would be best:

○ a. +"freshwater fishing" -catfish
○ b. -"freshwater fishing" +catfish
○ c. freshwater not catfish -fishing
○ d. fishing "freshwater not catfish"
○ e. (fish? -cat) + freshwater

14. Which of the following statements about journals is TRUE?

 ○ a. A journal contains research-oriented articles written by experts for a scholarly or professional audience.
 ○ b. Ramsey Library has no journals.
 ○ c. Every journal in Ramsey Library is on microfiche.
 ○ d. A journal usually includes articles on popular current topics for a general audience.
 ○ e. Books are much better than journal articles if you want up-to-date information.

15. You want to find articles on discipline in kindergarten, excluding everything that has to do with corporeal punishment. What would be the best Boolean search statement to use in an electronic database?

 ○ a. discipline AND NOT (kindergarten OR corporeal punishment)
 ○ b. (discipline OR kindergarten) AND corporeal punishment
 ○ c. discipline AND kindergarten AND corporeal punishment
 ○ d. (discipline AND NOT kindergarten) AND corporeal punishment
 ○ e. (discipline AND kindergarten) AND NOT corporeal punishment

16. Because Ramsey Library chooses to receive only those government documents that meet the needs of its community, it is known officially as:

 ○ a. a selective depository library.
 ○ b. a community government documents library.
 ○ c. a regional depository library.
 ○ d. an omni-depository library.
 ○ e. a government reference library.

17. You want to see what North Carolina state documents the library has about water pollution in the western part of the state.
You should search:

 ○ a. MarciveWeb DOCS.
 ○ b. the library catalog.
 ○ c. Yahoo!
 ○ d. InfoTrac.
 ○ e. General Statutes of North Carolina.

18. Study the following call numbers:

```
(a)  N      (b)  NC     (c)  ND     (d)  NK     (e)  NK
     17          3968        6           261         2614
     .B2         .T46        .J92        .P8         .H37
                 1974                    1991
```

A book with the call number **NK** would be on the shelf:
                                2614
                                .H9

○ a. before (a).
○ b. between (b) and (c).
○ c. between (c) and (d).
○ d. between (d) and (e).
○ e. after (e).

19. Which of the following is NOT housed in Ramsey Library's Special Collections?

○ a. Rare books
○ b. Back issues of the New York Times on microfilm.
○ c. Manuscripts
○ d. Oral histories
○ e. University Archives

20.

```
Chickens
              UF   Hens
              BT   Poultry
              NT   Game Fowl
                   Roosters
```

Based on the above entry from the Library of Congress Subject Headings,
     which of the following statements is CORRECT?

○ a. "Chickens" is not a valid subject heading. Use "Hens" instead.
○ b. Neither "Game fowl" nor "Roosters" is a valid subject heading.
○ c. The only valid subject heading listed is "Chickens."
○ d. "Hens" is a valid subject heading.
○ e. "Chickens," "Poultry," "Game Fowl," and "Roosters" are all valid subject
     headings.

21. You are using the library catalog to find books on "computer graphics." Your search retrieves more records than you want. Many of the books are at ASU and WCU. What is the best way to identify the books only at UNCA?

   ○ a. Use the Limit/Sort function and limit search results to the publication years 1990-1994 because all of the books at UNCA on this topic are very current.
   ○ b. Use the Limit/Sort function and limit where items are located to UNCA.
   ○ c. Since there is no way to limit search results, simply scan all titles retrieved and select those with a UNCA location symbol.
   ○ d. Do a Keyword search using the terms "UNCA computer graphics."
   ○ e. Do a Keyword search using the terms "computer graphics not ASU or WCU."

22. To perform a successful author search in the library catalog for Suzanne Fremon you may enter her name in all of the following ways EXCEPT:

   ○ a. Fremon, Suzanne
   ○ b. Fremon Suzanne
   ○ c. Suzanne Fremon
   ○ d. Fremon, Suz
   ○ e. Fremon S

23. Which of the following reference sources would be the best to use for answering the question: Where is the Ross Sea?

   ○ a. a concordance
   ○ b. a bibliography
   ○ c. Statistical Abstract of the United States
   ○ d. a gazetteer
   ○ e. a bio-bibliography

24. Articles in the periodical Sociological Quarterly may contain graphs or charts, but not photographs. The articles are written by researchers or experts in the field of sociology and related disciplines. The authors usually cite their sources in footnotes or reference lists. Sociology Quarterly is:

   ○ a. a scholarly journal.
   ○ b. a popular magazine.
   ○ c. a sensational magazine.
   ○ d. a periodical handbook.
   ○ e. an informative news/general interest magazine.

25. The ability to search more than one concept at a time is a major advantage of using:

   ○ a. an electronic index.
   ○ b. a microfilm index.
   ○ c. a printed index.
   ○ d. a microfiche index.
   ○ e. a card catalog.

26. The most efficient way to find magazines and journal **articles** on the subject you are researching is to:

  ○ a. use a handbook.
  ○ b. browse in the current periodical section.
  ○ c. use a periodical index.
  ○ d. use the Ramsey Library Periodicals Holdings List.
  ○ e. browse in the microfilm collection.

27. In doing research about mountain life, you used a book that you found in Ramsey Library. When you began to type the bibliography for your paper, you discovered that you hadn't written down all the information you needed about the book. Unfortunately, you have already turned in the book. You don't remember the author or the exact title, but you are sure that the words "snowbird" and "pie" were somewhere in the title. Which of the following searches on the library catalog would be the fastest way to relocate the book?

  ○ a. Call number search for F (the classification letter for material on mountain life)
  ○ b. Keyword search for snowbird and pie
  ○ c. Subject search for snowbirds
  ○ d. Title search for snowbird pie
  ○ e. Subject search for pie

28. The most efficient way to locate a copy of Clarice Lispector's short story "The Egg and the Chicken" is to:

  ○ a. check the library catalog for books by Clarice Lispector, then find the books and check the tables of contents in each one for the short story "The Egg and the Chicken."
  ○ b. look in a subject encyclopedia under the subject heading "Poultry.".
  ○ c. select the SHORT STORY search from the menu of the library catalog.
  ○ d. look in Short Story Index to find the title of a book that contains the story; then check the library catalog to see if Ramsey Library owns that book.
  ○ e. check the Biological and Agricultural Index for periodical articles on hens and egg production.

29.

```
Shakespeare quarterly
     Current issues on current periodical shelves.
     Microfilm: v. 1, 1950 - v. 15, 1964
     Bound: v. 14, 1963 - v. 30, 1979
     Microfilm: v. 31, 1980 - v. 45, 1995
     UNCA PERIODICAL  CALL NUMBER: PR2885 .S63
```

Based on the above entry from the Ramsey Library Periodical Holdings List, volume 24, 1973, of the periodical Shakespeare Quarterly is:

○ a. owned and at the bindery.
○ b. not owned by Ramsey Library.
○ c. owned and shelved in bound form at call number PR2885 .S63.
○ d. shelved on the current periodical shelves in call number location PR2885 .S63.
○ e. owned and available in microfilm.

30. **Does marijuana have a place in medicine?** Lisa Capaldina, Donald Tashkin, William Vilensky, Lori D. Talarico.
Patient Care Jan 30, 1998 v32 n2 p41(6)

Based on this entry from InfoTrac, which of the following statements is **FALSE**?

○ a. This article has four authors.
○ b. This article appears in the January 30, 1998 issue of Patient Care, Volume 32, number 2.
○ c. This article appears on p.41, column 6.
○ d. This article appears on p.41 and is 6 pages long.
○ e. The title of this article is "Does marijuana have a place in medicine?"

31.

```
KIDNEYS
   William S. Filler patents system using sound waves
to break up kidney stones and gallstones without
surgery (S), Ja 27,I,37:6
```

Based on the above citation from the 1990 New York Times Index, which of the following statements is **TRUE**?

○ a. An article by William S. Filler about using sound waves to break up kidney stones and gallstones appeared in the January 27 issue of the New York Times, in Section I, page 6, column 37.
○ b. An article about using sound waves to break up kidney stones and gallstones appeared in the New York Times in the (S)science section, January 27, Section 37, page 6.
○ c. (S)onic disruption of kidney stones and gallstones was first done successfully by William S. Filler on January 27th, according to the New York Times.
○ d. An article about William S. Filler's system of using sound waves to break up kidney stones and gallstones appeared in the January 27th issue of the New York Times in Section I, page 37 , column 6.
○ e. An article about using sound waves to break up kidney stones and gallstones appeared in the New York Times, Section S, page 6, column 37, January 27.

32. Of the following, which one is NOT primary source material for a paper on woman's suffrage in the United States?

○ a. A copy of the "Declaration of the Rights for Women" passed at the Women's Right's Convention in 1848.

○ b. An eyewitness account of the 1913 suffrage parade published in the Washington Post newspaper.

○ c. A summary and background article in American Women's History Encyclopedia.

○ d. The diary of Susan B. Anthony, a major leader of the suffrage movement.

○ e. The collected correspondence between Susan B. Anthony and Elizabeth Cady Stanton, an active suffragist.

33. You are interested in locating a kit or video on teaching science to first graders. What is the best way to determine that the library owns something that you can use?

○ a. Do a Subject search in the library catalog and limit results to the Education Collection.

○ b. Do a Keyword search on the library catalog and limit results to UNCA Reference Collection.

○ c. Do a Keyword search on the library catalog and limit results to UNCA Special Collections.

○ d. Do a Title search on the library catalog and limit results to UNCA science collection.

○ e. Do a Subject or Keyword search on the library catalog and limit results to UNCA Media Center.

Grade practice exam. Remember that you need to answer 74% of the questions correctly to pass the real final exam. You may want to print your results for review. By the way, your practice test results are not recorded for posterity.

Go back to the top.

 Ramsey Library

 UNCA home page

[http://bullpup.lib.unca.edu/library/lr/lr102/testsamp.html]

InfoTrail

InfoQuiz - Information Literacy Proficiency Quiz

Select Instructor from the list: | Instructor Name ▼ |

Select your class from the list: | Class Name ▼ |

Your Name:

Your Email:

In the questions below, choose the letter of the best answer(s).

1. Your professor has instructed you to research music and the Internet. You must decide which aspect of this topic you will focus on. Which of the following research questions is a good example of a suitably focused research question? **Choose one.**

○
  a. What effect has the Internet had on music sales in the last five years?

○
  b. Where is the best place on the Internet to buy music?

○
  c. Is there music on the Internet, and if so, how can I get it?

○
  d. Do musicians use the Internet?

2. What organization would probably have the most **comprehensive** information about current educational practices **across the state** of Colorado? **Choose one.**

○
  a. Colorado State Board of Education

○
  b. Local teacher's organization

○
  c. Your sixth grade teacher

○
  d. University's Education Department

3. Which of the following is a true statement. **Check all that apply.**

❑
a. Scholars usually make information available in published journals.

❑
b. Companies usually make information available on their Web sites.

❑
c. The U.S. Government usually makes information available in published journals.

❑
d. Organizations usually make information available on the Internet.

4. Which of the following resources **can** be accessed from the Library's Web page? **Check all that apply.**

❑
a. Tutorials

❑
b. Catalogs

❑
c. Full-text articles

❑
d. Periodical Indexes

❑
e. Library Tour

❑
f. Internet Search Engines

5. Which of the following can you **not** find for free on the Internet? **Choose one.**

○
a. Library Catalogs

○
b. Government Information

○
c. Subscription Periodical Indexes

○
d. Corporate Information

6. Which of the following materials are not listed in the USC Library's Catalog, Wolf Den? **Choose one.**

○
  a. Books

○
  b. Government Documents

○
  c. E-Books

○
  d. Videos

○
  e. Magazine Articles

7. If I wish to find books **by** William Faulkner in the U.S.C. Library, I would: **Choose one.**

○
  a. Determine the call number for American literature in the USC Floor Guide and browse the area until I find some.

○
  b. Browse by Author in Wolf Den, the USC library catalog.

○
  c. Perform an Keyword search in Wolf Den.

○
  d. Ask a friend where he found his books by William Faulkner.

8. You need to find a book **about** the author William Faulkner. Using Wolf Den, the USC Library Catalog, which type of search would locate what you need? **Choose one.**

○
  a. an author browse for Faulkner

○
  b. a title browse for the book The Sound and the Fury

○
  c. a subject browse for Faulkner

9. Which of the following information is included in the record for an item in Wolf Den? **Check all that are correct.**

❏
a. location

❏
b. title

❏
c. subject headings

❏
d. color

10. If an item in Wolf Den is listed as being in the "General Collection" and it has a call number of **PS3558 A7Z5C 1996**, on which floor would it be located? **Choose one.**

◯
a. 3rd

◯
b. 2nd

◯
c. 4th

11. The **most** efficient way to find magazine and journal articles on the subject you are researching is to: **Choose one.**

◯
a. check a printed index

◯
b. search an online periodical index for your topic

◯
c. find a bibliography on the topic

◯
d. browse the periodical shelves on the 3rd floor

12. The ability to search more than one concept at one time is a major advantage of using: **Choose one.**

◯
a. an electronic index

◯
b. a printed periodical index

◯
c. a citation index

◯
d. a subject encyclopedia

13. You are looking for journal articles on the topic of the Salem Witch Trials: which of the following Boolean searches would be most effective? **Choose One**.

○
 a. salem AND history

○
 b. salem AND witchcraft

○
 c. salem AND witch AND trials

○
 d. salem AND trials

14. You have found the following record in Academic Search Elite:

Subject(s): FEVER in Salem, A (Book)
Source: School Library Journal, Jun2000, Vol. 45[sic] Issue 6, p174, 1/6p
Author(s): Bercher, Peggy
Abstract: Reviews the book `A Fever in *Salem*: A New Interpretation of the New England Witch Trials,' by Laurie
   Winn Carlson.
AN: 3213985
ISSN: 0362-8930
Note: This title is held locally
Full Text Word Count: 232
Database: Academic Search Elite

View Item: ▤ Full Page Image   ▥ XML Full Text

Which of the following is true? **Choose One.**

○
 a. This article is not available online.

○
 b. This article is not available in the library.

○
 c. This article is available online, but not in the library.

○
 d. This article is available online and in the library.

15. You are researching the topic of *minorities AND television* for a research paper. On the Internet, you find a Web site that features the full text of a **popular magazine article** on the subject. In Academic Search Elite, you find an article entitled: "*Overrepresentation and underrepresentation of African Americans and Latinos as lawbreakers on local television news programs*", but the full text is not available in the USC library or online. Which of the following actions is more likely to help you retrieve appropriate information for a research paper? **Choose One.**

○
 a. Print the magazine article; it should be good enough. After all, it must be current if it is on the Internet.

○
 b. Request the Academic Search Elite article via Interlibrary Loan.

16. It is usually possible to find the following kinds of information for free on the Web. **Check all that apply.**

❑
  a. Financial information about companies

❑
  b. Addresses and phone numbers

❑
  c. Academic journal articles

❑
  d. Periodical Indexes

❑
  e. Current newspaper articles

17. I have found a web site on the Internet that has information about the subject that I am currently researching. Which statement is **TRUE? Choose One.**

○
  a. The information is accurate because it comes from an educational Web site

○
  b. The information needs to be carefully evaluated

○
  c. The information is better than information located in books

○
  d. This particular information will always be at this location address

18. Which **two** of the following choices do students commonly use to search the World Wide Web for sites on a research topic? **Choose Two.**

❑
  a. subject directories

❑
  b. spiders

❑
  c. search engines

❑
  d. tutorials

19. Which of the following are clues that a Web site is a "good" site to use for research? **Check all that apply.**

❑
  a. The site lists the date it was last updated

❑
  b. The site seems to have scholarly information

❑
  c. The site provides a link back to its' sponsoring organization

❑
  d. The name of the author of the site is given

❑
  e. The site provides a bibliography

20. The USC Library Reference Desk, where you can always come for help or information is located on which floor of the library? **Choose One.**

◯
  a. 1st floor

◯
  b. 2nd floor

◯
  c. 3rd floor

Submit	Reset

[http://library.uscolo.edu/infotrail/quiz1.html]

West Texas A & M University

Final Exam
Fundamentals of Library Research
Due May 3, 2001

This is a take-home exam. You must turn it in to me by 3:30 on May 3rd. The exam can be turned in earlier. I encourage you to complete it as soon as possible so that you can focus on studying for your other exams. Please leave your exam with the librarian at the Reference Desk if I am not here and ask that it be put on my desk. Be sure to keep a copy for yourself.

Please type your answers. Indicate which question you are answering. **You must return these exam question pages to me.**

You must also turn in the printed search screens so I can see how you did your search. The way in which you do your search is as important as the correct answer to the question. Read the question at least two times. Underline important words. **If you do not turn in the printed search screens, you will lose half of the points for the question.**

The first four questions are worth 25 points. The fifth question is an extra credit question worth 10 points. You must complete the first four questions to receive extra credit. In other words, if you do not finish the first four questions, don't waste time with the fifth one. Answer all parts of each question?

If you have questions about the exam, ask me and only me. Do not ask Library staff or anyone else for assistance other than asking for a book that might be at the Reference Desk. Do not work with your classmates. That is cheating and will result in an F. Each of you has different questions.

Take your time. Read the questions carefully. Think about the most logical way to do the search before you begin. That should save you time and result in a better grade.

Good luck!!!!!!

1. **Cornette Library owns the 7th edition of Black's Law Dictionary. You will need to use the book to find the answers to questions d and e.**

    a. Search the appropriate access tool to answer questions b and c. What is this access tool?
    b. In what area of the Library is this book located?
    c. What is its call number?
    d. What is the definition of *gubernator navis*?
    e. What word are you directed to see if you look under *nonrecourse loan*?

2. **Find a book in Cornette Library about brickwork in Italy. Do not look at the book for the information to answer the following questions. Instead view the full record for this book in the access tool you used to find the information.**

    a. What is its title?
    b. Who is the main author of this book?
    c. When was it published and by whom?
    d. List the subject headings for this book.
    e. Does this book include a bibliography?
    f. Where is the book located and what is its call number?
    g. What access tool did you use to find this information?

3. **Use the database PsycINFO for this question. Find an article about telepathy and empathy published in Perceptual & Motor Skills. The author is James M. Donovan.**

    a. Write down the information you would need to cite this article.
    b. Where does the author work?
    c. What is the hypothesis examined in this article?
    d. Does Cornette Library own the issue of the journal where this article appears? If so, in which Periodicals area is it located?

4. **Use GPO Monthly Catalog to find a government document published after 1998 on flood insurance in the city of Ponchatoula in Tangipahoa Parish, Louisiana.**

    a. What is the title?
    b. Name the publisher and its location?
    c. When was the document published?
    d. List a subject heading (descriptor)?
    e. What is the SuDoc (GovDoc) number for this document?
    f. Does Cornette Library own this document? How do you know?

EXTRA CREDIT QUESTION

Go to Librarians' Index to the Internet to find a Web site specifically on Margaret Sanger.

1. What is the title of this Web site? What is the URL for this Web site?
2. What do interns working on the electronic edition project do?
3. Give the title of one birth control book written by Margaret Sanger. When was it written?

DOCUMENTS :
Evaluation of Library Instruction: General

JAMES EARL CARTER LIBRARY
Georgia Southwestern State University

Library Instruction Evaluation Form

Class: _____

Time and date: _____

Instructor: _____

Librarian: _____

1. The objectives of the instruction session were clearly and effectively stated.

   ___strongly agree   ___agree   ___disagree   ___strongly disagree   ___N/A

2. The librarian covered the right amount of information for the length of the session.

   ___strongly agree   ___agree   ___disagree   ___strongly disagree   ___N/A

3. The information presented was well organized and clearly presented.

   ___strongly agree   ___agree   ___disagree   ___strongly disagree   ___N/A

4. Good examples and illustrations were used in the presentation.

   ___strongly agree   ___agree   ___disagree   ___strongly disagree   ___N/A

5. I learned something about using the online catalog during the session.

   ___strongly agree   ___agree   ___disagree   ___strongly disagree   ___N/A

6. I learned something about finding journal articles during the session.

   ___strongly agree   ___agree   ___disagree   ___strongly disagree   ___N/A

7. I can use the library's resources more effectively now.

   ___strongly agree   ___agree   ___disagree   ___strongly disagree   ___N/A

8. I will be comfortable asking for assistance in the library.

   ___ trongly agree   ___agree   ___disagree   ___strongly disagree   ___N/A

9. Overall, the library instruction session was useful.

   ___strongly agree   ___agree   ___disagree   ___strongly disagree   ___N/A

Additional comments about this instruction session:

Thank you for taking the time to fill-out the evaluation form. We appreciate your assistance.

LIBRARY RESEARCH SURVEY

PART 1
Use the following designations to respond to these statements:

N = This item was NEW material to you
+ = This item was HELPFUL reinforcement of something you had been taught previously
O = This item was an unnecessary rehash of OLD material

That's an N for NEW, + for HELPFUL, and O for OLD:

_____The Library of Congress classification (call number) system

_____Using appropriate general and specialized encyclopedias

_____Using red LC Subject Headings books to seek subject headings and related terms

_____Doing keyword and Boolean searches on GRACE

_____Doing a subject search on GRACE with LC subject headings

_____Determining and locating appropriate indexes for a periodical search

_____Using print periodical indexes

_____Using electronic indexes and databases

_____Locating newspaper articles

_____Determining availability of the full text of periodical articles, in various formats

_____Evaluating a periodical to determine if it is scholarly or popular

_____Practicing correct bibliographical form (APA, MLA, Turabian)

_____Critical assessment of Web-based information

_____Awareness of sources for current data (Statistical Abstracts, Facts on File, almanacs, etc.)

_____Locating information to determine author credibility.

(OVER)

_____Awareness of sources for accessing items in anthologies (<u>Granger's</u> <u>Index</u> <u>to</u> <u>Poetry</u>,

<u>Short</u> <u>Story</u> <u>Index</u>, etc.)

PART 2
Please make brief comments on the following items.

    A. The classroom presentations

    B. The assignments

    C. Library Research Sessions Web page (organization, availability of materials)

What changes would you suggest in this course? Be specific.

Have the skills that you learned in these sessions benefited you in other classes? Why or why not?

Do you have other comments relevant to the class or the instructor?

EVALUATION OF ENGLISH 101 LIBRARY ORIENTATION

Please fill out this evaluation form and **do not sign it**. You may return it to one of the librarians or to the circulation desk in the lobby. Thank you.

1. Evaluate your knowledge of the library **before** these orientation classes.

	EXCELLENT	GOOD	ADEQUATE	KNEW LITTLE	KNEW NOTHING
InfoTrac (DISCUS)	1	2	3	4	5
New York Times Index	1	2	3	4	5
OPAC (on-line catalog)	1	2	3	4	5
Periodical Indexes	1	2	3	4	5
Reference Books	1	2	3	4	5

2. Evaluate your knowledge of the library **after** these orientation classes.

	EXCELLENT	GOOD	ADEQUATE	KNEW LITTLE	KNEW NOTHING
InfoTrac (DISCUS)	1	2	3	4	5
New York Times Index	1	2	3	4	5
OPAC (on-line catalog)	1	2	3	4	5
Periodical Indexes	1	2	3	4	5
Reference Books	1	2	3	4	5

3. Did the use of exercises each day help? _____ Yes _____ No

4. Which day or days were most useful to you?

> _____ All
> _____ InfoTrac (DISCUS)
> _____ New York Times Index
> _____ OPAC (on-line catalog)
> _____ Periodical Indexes
> _____ Reference Books

5. Do you feel free to ask one of the librarians for help now? _____ Yes _____ No

6. Any comments that you wish to make concerning the classes (how to improve them, what else would have been helpful, etc.) would be appreciated.

Lynchburg College
Knight-Capron Library_____**Database Guide**

Library Instructional Session – Student Evaluation

We would appreciate it if you would help us to assess the effectiveness of our Library Instruction program. Please take a few minutes to answer the following questions. Your responses will be used to improve our instruction program. Feel free to write additional comments. Thank you.

Course number and section:_____ Date_____

Library Instructor:_____

Please circle the appropriate response.

1. The information in the library presentation covered the kinds of sources that I need to complete my specific assignment.

Strongly disagree   Strongly agree
1. . . . .2. . . . .3. . . . .4. 5

2. The resource examples and handouts were appropriate for my information needs for this course.

Strongly disagree   Strongly agree
1. . . . .2. . . . .3. . . . .4. 5

3. The presentation was well organized.

Strongly disagree   Strongly agree
1. . . . .2. . . . .3. . . . .4. 5

4. The session presented sufficient information about available online resources for me to begin my research.

Strongly disagree   Strongly agree
1. . . . .2. . . . .3. . . . .4. 5

5. There was adequate time for hands on practice during the session.

Strongly disagree   Strongly agree
1. . . . .2. . . . .3. . . . .4. 5

6. The overall quality of the library presentation given to my class was:

Poor. . . . . . . Fair. . . . . . . Good . . . . Very good . . . . Excellent

7. The thing I liked most about this presentation was:

8. In future sessions, coverage of the following could be eliminated:

9. What could be done to insure a better presentation next time? (Examples: timing of the class, additional information resources, in-class worksheets.)

10. Indicate the degree to which you would agree with the following statements:

As a result of this session, I feel that I:

a. obtained a good understanding of the information gathering and research process.

Strongly disagree   Strongly agree
1. . . . .2. . . . .3. . . . .4. 5

b. increased my knowledge of library and information resources and services.

Strongly disagree   Strongly agree
1. . . . .2. . . . .3. . . . .4. 5

c. will be able to carry out the assignments for this class at a higher level of achievement.

Strongly disagree   Strongly agree
1. . . . .2. . . . .3. . . . .4. 5

d. am better prepared for work in other classes.

Strongly disagree   Strongly agree
1. . . . .2. . . . .3. . . . .4. 5

University of St. Thomas Libraries

Bibliographic Instruction Evaluation Form

Course_____   Date_____

Class: FR____   Soph____   Jr_____   Sr____   Grad_____   Other_____

Please circle your response:

	Strong agree			Strongly disagree		

1. The library presentation increased my confidence   1   2   3   4   5
   in using the library.

2. The presentation will be/was useful in helping me   1   2   3   4   5
   find and use information resources.

3. The instructional materials used in the presentation   1   2   3   4   5
   were/will be useful in completing my research.
   (Use those appropriate.)

   Handouts   1   2   3   4   5   N/A

   Videos   1   2   3   4   5   N/A

   Overheads   1   2   3   4   5   N/A

   Computer examples   1   2   3   4   5   N/A

   Computer hands-on activities   1   2   3   4   5   N/A

   Why or why not?

4. The facilities (instruction room, computers
   equipment, etc.) were adequate.   1   2   3   4   5

5. What was the most valuable thing you learned in the library instructional session?

6. Any other comments:

Library Instruction Evaluation

Please help us evaluate this workshop by answering the questions below and adding your comments.

Participant: (Circle one)
Freshman   Sophomore   Junior   Senior   Graduate   Faculty

Date of Class:_____Time of day:_____

Your Course Instructor:_____Title of Class:_____

Library Instructor:_____

I've attended a library instruction class before: (Circle one)   Yes   No

I had a specific assignment to accomplish in conjunction with this presentation.
(Circle one)   Yes   No

My Professor participated in this session.(Circle one)   Yes   No

(Circle one)	Strongly Agree	Moderately Agree	Slightly Agree	Slightly Disagree	Moderately Disagree	Strongly Disagree
This presentation helped me learn how to start my research.	6	5	4	3	2	1
The presentation was clear.	6	5	4	3	2	1
The hands-on experience will help me to complete my assignment.	6	5	4	3	2	1
The librarian treated each student with respect.	6	5	4	3	2	1

The most important thing that I learned was: **(Choose one)**
    How to locate a journal article or a book on my topic. _____
    How to access the library's web page databases.   _____
    How to use Interlibrary Loan to get my information. _____
    How to decide which databases I should use.   _____
    How to search the Internet more efficiently.   _____

I would have like to learn more about:

_____

Comments or suggestions:

_____

Thank you for your input. Could we contact you for more information?
(Circle one)   Yes   No
If so, please give us your e-mail address._____

Whitworth College Library

INSTRUCTION EVALUATION

Instructions: Please circle the number that corresponds with your level of agreement with each statement. Use this scale:

1=Disagree   2=Disagree Somewhat   3=Agree Somewhat   4=Agree   NC=Not Covered

Research Strategy Coverage

1. I realize the value of learning research in a step-by-step, organized way.   1   2   3   4   NC

2. I can describe effective ways of conducting a research strategy   1   2   3   4   NC

3. I understand the use of reference sources to define a topic and lead me to other resources.   1   2   3   4   NC

4. I can effectively use computerized library catalogs and indices. 1   2   3   4   NC

5. I understand how to use keywords and subject headings to perform thorough subject searches.   1   2   3   4   NC

6. I understand how to locate books in a library.   1   2   3   4   NC

7. I understand how to use periodical indices to find journal articles.   1   2   3   4   NC

8. I understand how to locate internet sites appropriate for research.   1   2   3   4   NC

9. I understand how to evaluate internet resources that I can cite in my bibliography.   1   2   3   4   NC

Library Presentation

1. The instructor was clear and informative.   1   2   3   4
2. The class was taught at my level of understanding.   1   2   3   4
3. I understood the majority of the material in the presentation. 1   2   3   4

4. The information presented was relevant and useful.   1   2   3   4

5. Examples were adequate to illustrate concepts taught in class.   1   2   3   4

6. The instructor was open to questions and seemed helpful
    in general.   1   2   3   4

7. The instruction was applicable to the class assignments.   1   2   3   4

8. I would recommend this instruction to other students.   1   2   3   4

Applying the Research Strategy:

1. The reference librarians are helpful.   1   2   3   4   NC

Comments:

[Developer/Contact: Tami Echavarria (techavarria@whitworth.edu)]

DOCUMENTS :
Evaluation of Library Instruction: Evaluation by Faculty

Eastern Washington University

Course:_____

Date:_____

Library Instruction Feedback Form

Please complete this form immediately after the session so we can evaluate and improve our instructional program. Your comments and suggestions are important to us. Thank you.

Please indicate your status: (circle one)   Faculty   Instructor   Teaching Assistant

1. The scheduling and preplanning activities (such as setting goals and objectives, allowing adequate time for sessions, etc.) for the library instruction session were: (circle one)
Excellent   Good   Fair   Poor

Comments:

2. The content of the instructional session was: (circle one)
Excellent   Good   Fair   Poor

Comments:

3. The library instructor's effectiveness in teaching the subject matter was: (circle one)
Excellent   Good   Fair   Poor

Comments:

4. Is there anything else that you would like to have had covered in this or future instructional sessions?
Comments:

_____

Bibliographic instructor's comments:

Adopted by Library faculty 6/3/97

emerson college library

Library Instruction Session Evaluation

During this past academic year you brought a class into the Library's Electronic Classroom for a research and instruction Session. Please help us assess the value of this program by answering a few questions about the session and your class.

Why did you request an instruction session at the library

What was valuable about the instruction session?

How did student work reflect the concepts emphasized in the instruction session?

Would you request a library instruction session again?

Thank you for taking the time to answer these questions. If you have any questions, or would like to make any additional comments, please feel free to contact Anna Litten, Coordinator of Library Instruction, at ext. 8330 or anna_litten@emerson.edu

Faculty Evaluation of Library Instruction

Your Name:

Date:

Thank you for completing this form. Feel free to use space below each item for additional comments or examples.

Librarian

The librarian was well prepared	Strongly Agree	Agree	Disagree	Strongly Disagree	N/A

The librarian was knowledgeable about my students' needs	Strongly Agree	Agree	Disagree	Strongly Disagree	N/A

The librarian explained the relationship between the presentation content and the class assignment	Strongly Agree	Agree	Disagree	Strongly Disagree	N/A

The librarian used terms and examples my class could understand	Strongly Agree	Agree	Disagree	Strongly Disagree	N/A

The librarian was receptive to questions/discussion	Strongly Agree	Agree	Disagree	Strongly Disagree	N/A

The Library Session

The library instruction session(s) met my expectations for the course	Strongly Agree	Agree	Disagree	Strongly Disagree	N/A

Session content was appropriate for level of class	Strongly Agree	Agree	Disagree	Strongly Disagree	N/A

Session content was coordinated/planned with me	Strongly Agree	Agree	Disagree	Strongly Disagree	N/A

Session content was appropriate to class assignment	Strongly Agree	Agree	Disagree	Strongly Disagree	N/A

Session content made good use of time allotted	Strongly Agree	Agree	Disagree	Strongly Disagree	N/A

Other comments:

Please return this form to the librarian following the session, **or** mail to Katherine Furlong, Campus Box 420. Thank You!

End-of-Semester
Faculty Evaluation of Library Instruction

Your Name:

Date:

Thank you for scheduling library instruction this semester. To continuously improve our program, we ask that you complete this evaluation. Please feel free to include additional comments or examples.

Outcomes of Library Session

The library instruction session(s) served the purpose I intended for the class	*Strongly Agree*	*Agree*	*Disagree*	*Strongly Disagree*	*N/A*
The library instruction session was a valuable experience for my students	*Strongly Agree*	*Agree*	*Disagree*	*Strongly Disagree*	*N/A*
My students' assignments and papers showed a **more extensive** use of source material	*Strongly Agree*	*Agree*	*Disagree*	*Strongly Disagree*	*N/A*
My students' assignments and papers showed a greater **quality** in use of source material	*Strongly Agree*	*Agree*	*Disagree*	*Strongly Disagree*	*N/A*
I would schedule library instruction sessions for future classes	*Strongly Agree*	*Agree*	*Disagree*	*Strongly Disagree*	*N/A*
I would recommend course-integrated library instruction to other faculty members.	*Strongly Agree*	*Agree*	*Disagree*	*Strongly Disagree*	*N/A*

Other comments:

Please return this form to Katherine Furlong, Campus Box 420. Thank You!

Lynchburg College
Knight-Capron **Library**_____ *INSTRUCTIONAL SERVICES*

<u>Faculty Evaluation of Library Instructional Session</u>

The Instructional Services Office of Knight-Capron Library would appreciate it if you would help us to assess the effectiveness of our Library Instruction program. Please take a few minutes to answer the following questions. Your responses will be used to improve our instruction program. Feel free to write additional comments. Thank you.

Course number and section: _____ Date: _____

Library Instructor:_____

<u>Please circle the appropriate response</u>.

1. The range and amount of content presented were appropriate for students taking this class.
    a. Strongly agree
    b. Agree
    c. Neutral/Undecided
    d. Disagree
    e. Strongly disagree

2. The resource examples and handouts were appropriate for the needs of my class.

    a. Strongly agree
    b. Agree
    c. Neutral/Undecided
    d. Disagree
    e. Strongly disagree

3. The presentation included the information needed by my students to complete their library-related assignment.

    a. Strongly agree
    b. Agree
    c. Neutral/Undecided
    d. Disagree
    e. Strongly disagree

4. The teaching format of this library presentation was appropriate for the topic and needs of my students.

    a. Strongly agree

    b. Agree

    c. Neutral/Undecided

    d. Disagree

    e. Strongly disagree

5. The presentation was well organized.

    a. Strongly agree

    b. Agree

    c. Neutral/Undecided

    d. Disagree

    e. Strongly disagree

6. My objectives for this session were to enable my students to (check all that apply).

    a. understand basic services

    b. learn the range of key reference resources in my discipline

    c. obtain in-depth knowledge of a particular electronic resource

    d. develop effective search strategies for information resources

    e. learn how to evaluate the quality and reliability of information resources

    f. become familiar with the library facility

    g. other_____

7. To what degree did this session meet your expectations?

    a. Exceeded expectations

    b. Met expectations

    c. Met expectations somewhat

    d. Not at all

8. The overall quality of the library presentation given to my class(es) was:

    a. Excellent

    b. Very good

    c. Good

    d. Fair

    e. Poor

9. The thing I liked most about this presentation was:

10. In future sessions, coverage of the following could be eliminated:

11. What could be done to insure a better presentation next time? (examples: timing of the class, additional information resources, in-class worksheets.)

Ursuline College

Dear Faculty Member,

You have recently brought a class to Besse Library for a special session. Would you please take a moment to fill out this evaluation sheet and return it to Betsey Belkin in the library.

Besse Library Session Evaluation

Your Name_____ Department _____
Date of Session_____ Class_____
Library Instructor's Name _____

	Needs Improvement	Satisfactory	Very Good
Organization of Session			
Effectiveness of Presentation			
Comfortable Pace			
Instructor's Knowledge of Topic			
Quality/Relevance of Visuals			
Usefulness of Handouts			
Potential impact on student research			

How could this session have been improved?

Do you think you will return for a session with another class?

Other Comments.

DOCUMENTS :
Evaluation of Library Instruction:
Evaluation of Instructor

Evaluation of Instructor

Instructor:

Date:

Please complete as completely as possible. Feel free to use space below each item for additional comments or examples.

Introduction

Successfully captured the audience	Strongly Agree	Agree	Neutral	Disagree	Strongly Disagree	N/A
Clearly stated purpose of session	Strongly Agree	Agree	Neutral	Disagree	Strongly Disagree	N/A
Related purpose to class assignment/faculty goals	Strongly Agree	Agree	Neutral	Disagree	Strongly Disagree	N/A
Convinced audience of importance to listen and participate	Strongly Agree	Agree	Neutral	Disagree	Strongly Disagree	N/A

Content

Made session relevant to audience need by showing implications and applications	Strongly Agree	Agree	Neutral	Disagree	Strongly Disagree	N/A
Explained the relationship between content of presentation and class assignment	Strongly Agree	Agree	Neutral	Disagree	Strongly Disagree	N/A
Adapted easily to changing content/situation	Strongly Agree	Agree	Neutral	Disagree	Strongly Disagree	N/A
Used terms and examples audience could understand	Strongly Agree	Agree	Neutral	Disagree	Strongly Disagree	N/A
Made content appropriate to level of class	Strongly Agree	Agree	Neutral	Disagree	Strongly Disagree	N/A
Made content appropriate to class assignment	Strongly Agree	Agree	Neutral	Disagree	Strongly Disagree	N/A
Made content appropriate to time allotted	Strongly Agree	Agree	Neutral	Disagree	Strongly Disagree	N/A
Coordinated/planned content with faculty	Strongly Agree	Agree	Neutral	Disagree	Strongly Disagree	N/A

Delivery

Presented content in clear, under-standable and organized manner	Strongly Agree	Agree	Neutral	Disagree	Strongly Disagree	N/A
Encouraged and facilitated class discussion	Strongly Agree	Agree	Neutral	Disagree	Strongly Disagree	N/A
Asked for student and faculty input	Strongly Agree	Agree	Neutral	Disagree	Strongly Disagree	N/A
Adapted teaching methods to address learning styles of audience	Strongly Agree	Agree	Neutral	Disagree	Strongly Disagree	N/A
Spoke at appropriate speed; varied voice tone, spoke loud enough	Strongly Agree	Agree	Neutral	Disagree	Strongly Disagree	N/A
Maintained eye contact with audience	Strongly Agree	Agree	Neutral	Disagree	Strongly Disagree	N/A
Handled visual aids and technology smoothly	Strongly Agree	Agree	Neutral	Disagree	Strongly Disagree	N/A
Used movement strategically; had appropriate gestures	Strongly Agree	Agree	Neutral	Disagree	Strongly Disagree	N/A
Used handout(s) effectively	Strongly Agree	Agree	Neutral	Disagree	Strongly Disagree	N/A
Was free of distracting fillers or mannerisms	Strongly Agree	Agree	Neutral	Disagree	Strongly Disagree	N/A
Showed respect to all participants	Strongly Agree	Agree	Neutral	Disagree	Strongly Disagree	N/A
Handled difficult situations with poise	Strongly Agree	Agree	Neutral	Disagree	Strongly Disagree	N/A

Conclusion

Reviewed main points	Strongly Agree	Agree	Neutral	Disagree	Strongly Disagree	N/A
Encouraged follow-up contact	Strongly Agree	Agree	Neutral	Disagree	Strongly Disagree	N/A
Made good use of allotted time	Strongly Agree	Agree	Neutral	Disagree	Strongly Disagree	N/A
Closed with impact and finality	Strongly Agree	Agree	Neutral	Disagree	Strongly Disagree	N/A

What advice would you give to this instructor to improve his/her presentation skills?

Other comments: kaf 5/2/02

Rating Guide

Directions: Respond to each of the statements below by writing next to the statement the number which best expresses your judgment.

> 1.= Strength
> 2.= Somewhat of a Problem
> 3.= A Major Problem
> 4.= Not Applicable

Content: Importance and Suitability

_____ The material presented is generally accepted by colleagues to be worth knowing.

_____ The material presented is important for this group of students.

_____ The instructor seemed to match the lecture material to the students' backgrounds.

_____ The examples used were easily understood by students.

_____ When appropriate, a distinction was made between factual material and opinions.

_____ Appropriate authorities were cited to support statements.

_____ When appropriate, divergent viewpoints were presented.

_____ A sufficient amount of material was included in the lecture.

Other Comments:

Content: Organization

Introduction:

_____Stated the purpose of the lecture.

_____Presented a brief overview of the lecture content.

_____Stated a problem to be solved or discussed during the lecture.

_____Made explicit the relationship between today's and the previous lecture.

Body of Lecture:

_____Asked questions periodically to determine whether too much or too little information was being presented.

_____Presented examples, illustrations or graphics to clarify abstract and difficult ideas.

_____Explicitly stated the relationships among various ideas in the lecture.

_____Periodically summarized the most important ideas in the lecture.

Conclusion:

_____Solved or otherwise dealt with any problems raised during the lecture.

_____Restated what students were expected to gain from the lecture material.

_____Summarized the main ideas in the lecture.

_____Related the day's lecture to upcoming presentations.

Other Comments:

Presentation: Style

Introduction:

_____Voice could be easily heard.
_____Voice was raised or lowered for variety and emphasis.
_____Speech was neither too formal nor too casual.
_____Speech fillers, ("okay now," "ahm,") were not distracting.
_____Rate of speech was neither too fast nor too slow.

Non-Verbal Communication:

_____Established and maintained eye contact with the class as lecture began.
_____Listened carefully to students' comments and questions.
_____Wasn't too stiff and formal in appearance.
_____Wasn't too casual in appearance.
_____Facial and body movements were consistent with instructor's intentions. For example, the instructor looked at students while waiting for their responses after asking questions.

Other Comments:

Presentation: Clarity

_____Stated the purpose at the beginning of the lecture.
_____Defined new terms, concepts and principles.
_____Told the students why certain processes, techniques or formulas were used to solve problems.
_____Used relevant examples to explain major ideas.
_____Used clear and simple examples.
_____Explicitly related new ideas to familiar ones.
_____Reiterated definitions of new terms to help students become accustomed to them.
_____Provided occasional summaries and restatements of important ideas.
_____Used alternate explanations when necessary.
_____Slowed the word flow when ideas were complex and difficult.
_____Did not often digress from the main topic.
_____Talked to the class, not to the board or windows.
_____The board work appeared organized and legible.

Other Comments:

Questioning Skills

_____Asked questions to see what the students knew about the lecture topic.
_____Addressed questions to individual students as well as the group at large.
_____Used rhetorical questions to gain students' attention.
_____Paused after all questions to allow students time to think of an answer.
_____Encouraged students to answer diffi-cult questions by providing cues or rephrasing.
_____When necessary, asked students to clarify their questions.
_____Asked probing questions if a student's answer was incomplete or superficial.
_____Repeated answers when necessary so the entire class could hear.
_____Received students' questions politely and when possible enthusiastically.
_____Requested that questions which required time-consuming answers of limited interest be discussed before or after class or during office hours.

Other Comments:

Establishing and Maintaining Contact with Students

Establishing Contact:

_____Greeted students with a bit of small talk.
_____Established eye contact with as many students as possible.
_____Set ground rules for student partici-pation and questioning.
_____Used questions to gain student attention.
_____Encouraged student questions.

Maintaining Contact:

_____Maintained eye contact with as many students as possible.
_____Used rhetorical questions to re-engage student attention.
_____Asked questions which allowed the instructor to gauge students' progress.
_____Was able to answer students' questions satisfactorily.
_____Noted and responded to signs of puzzlement, boredom, curiosity, etc.
_____Varied the pace of the lecture to keep students alert.
_____Spoke at a rate which allowed students time to take notes.

Other Comments:

From: **IMPROVING YOUR LECTURING**
Nancy A. Diamond & Greg Sharp, Course Development Division; John C. Ory, Measurement   and Research Division
Revised 1983: Luisette Behmer, Nancy Diamond, Marne Helgesen, Greg Sharp, Richard Smock,
  Course Development Division
URL: http://www.oir.uiuc.edu/did/imaterials/LECTURE/Lecture4.htm (Accessed: 04/22/02)

DOCUMENTS :
Evaluation of Library Instruction: Other

Evaluation Form

We need your comments! Tell us what you think about the tutorial. Your opinions will help us improve it.

Name: (optional)

E-Mail Address: (optional)

1. Your Status:

- ◌ Freshman

- ◌ Sophomore

- ◌ Junior

- ◌ Senior

- ◌ Graduate Student

- ◌ Other

2. Was the material well organized and clearly presented?

- ◌ Well organized

- ◌ Adequately organized

- ◌ Inadequately organized

- ◌ Badly organized

Comments:

3. How many of the sections of the tutorial did you complete?

    ◌ All

    ◌ 5

    ◌ 3 or 4

    ◌ 1 or 2

    ◌ None

4. What did you like about this tutorial?

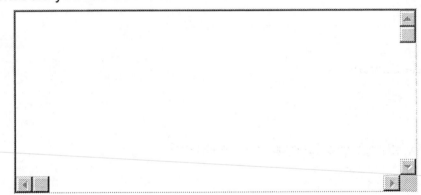

5. How could this tutorial be improved?

6. How long did you spend on the tutorial?

   ○   1 - 15 minutes

   ○   15 - 30 minutes

   ○   30 - 45 minutes

   ○   45 - 60 minutes

   ○   More than 1 hour

   ○   More than 2 hours

7. Additional comments (can be about the tutorial or anything regarding the library):

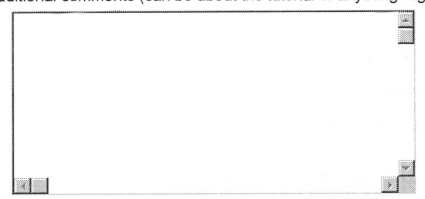

THANK YOU!!! Please click on the Submit button below.

http://ocfrontpage.otterbein.edu/library/usereval.htm

Evaluation of NEON Instructional Web Page for (*insert course name here*)
Refer to the attached copy of the web page for your course

1.   ___ I used one or more NEON databases listed at the top of the page.

2.   The most useful of the NEON databases was:

3.   ___ I used one or more of the web sites listed on the bottom half of the page.

4.   The most useful web site on the page was:

5.   After using some of the sources on the web page, I still needed information about:

6.   Where I found information from other sources:

   ___ Printed indexes

   ___ Books

   ___ From other people

   ___ Other web sites

   ___ Other sources (describe):

7.   I would rate the web page for this course as:

   Very useful   Moderately useful   Not useful at all
          1   2   3

8.   I would rate the library instruction for this course as:

   Very useful   Moderately useful   Not useful at all
          1   2   3

9.   Suggestions & comments:

   http://www2.library.unr.edu/ragains/assess.html > Student Reactions to Library
   Instruction > University of Nevada, Reno Libraries. Student Evaluation Form

Schmidt Library
York College of Pennsylvania

Spring 2000
IFL 101 Exit Survey

Student Name: Section:
                                                 Instructor:

1. What is your attitude toward computers? (You can have more than one answer.)

☐ Uncomfortable   ☐ Useful   ☐ Addicted
☐ Would like to know more ☐ Fun

2. Do you feel your competency and comfort level with computers has increased this semester?

Competency   ☐ Yes   ☐ No

Comfort level ☐ Yes   ☐ No

3. Where do you usually access a computer: (Check all that apply.)

☐ Home   ☐ Campus computer lab   ☐ Other (specify)
☐ Dorm   ☐ Work   _____

4. Please rank your top three uses of the computer:

Email/chat/bulletin/newsgroups   _____
Word processing   _____
Net surfing   _____
Research/information   _____
Games   _____
Other (specify)   _____

5. Do you know the difference between:

Popular and scholarly sources?   ☐ Yes   ☐ No
Primary and secondary sources?   ☐ Yes   ☐ No
Subject and keyword searching?   ☐ Yes   ☐ No
Web directories and search engines?   ☐ Yes   ☐ No
Computer literacy and information literacy?   ☐ Yes   ☐ No

Please respond to the following questions according to your actual experiences with the topic:

1 - no knowledge   3 - working knowledge
2 - somewhat familiar   4 - very familiar, use regularly

---

6.   Please rate your knowledge of :

Researching a topic	1	2	3	4
Searching for books in an online catalog	1	2	3	4
Searching for AV items in an online catalog	1	2	3	4
Searching for periodical articles in an online index	1	2	3	4
Searching for reference sources (encyclopedias, dictionaries, handbooks, etc.)	1	2	3	4
Searching the Internet for quality information	1	2	3	4
Evaluating the quality of the resources you find	1	2	3	4
Using Boolean (and, or, not) search techniques	1	2	3	4

7. How would you rate your general computer knowledge?   1   2   3   4

8. Please rate your knowledge of the following operating system:

Windows	1	2	3	4

9. Please rate your knowledge of the following programs or library systems:

Word processing	1	2	3	4
Internet	1	2	3	4
Email/chat/bulletin/newsgroups	1	2	3	4
CD-ROM	1	2	3	4
Library online catalogs	1	2	3	4
Games	1	2	3	4

10. Please rate your knowledge of these specific programs:

Microsoft Word	1	2	3	4
PowerPoint	1	2	3	4
Netscape or other Internet browsers	1	2	3	4

UST Library Instruction Feedback

Course name and number_____ _____
_____ First-year student   _____ Sophomore   _____ Junior   _____ Senior
_____ Graduate student   _____ Other

1. Were the library handouts passed out in class useful for your course research? (Circle One)

    Not useful   Very Useful
          1   2   3   4   5

2. Were the research strategies discussed in the library presentation useful for your research? (Circle One)

    Not useful   Very Useful
          1   2   3   4   5

3. Did you schedule an appointment with a librarian to help you with your research?
    _____ Yes   _____ No, do you wish you had done so? _____

    If yes, what was most useful about your research appointment?

4. Which library resources did you use for your research? (Circle all that apply.)

    Reference books   Electronic journals/magazines   Library books

    Print Indexes   Electronic/Web-based indexes   Reference Desk/Library Staff

    Web/Internet   Print journals/magazines   Other _____

5. What were the most useful library resources for your research? Why?

6. How much of the information presented in the library instruction did you already know? (Circle One)

    All   None
          1   2   3   4   5

7. What would you like to know about library research?

Use back of sheet for additional comments
Thanks!

University of St. Thomas

UST Library Research Feedback

Course name and number_____
_____ First-year student   _____ Sophomore   _____ Junior   _____ Senior
_____ Graduate student   _____ Other

1. Did you use any library help guides, documentation, or information sheets for your course research?

    _____ Yes   _____ No

    If yes, were they useful? (Circle One)

    Not useful   Very Useful
      1   2   3   4   5

2. Did you schedule an appointment with a librarian to help you with your research?

    _____ Yes   _____ No.   Do you wish you had done so? _____

    If yes, what was most useful about your research appointment?

3. Which library resources did you use for your research? (Circle all that apply.)

Reference books	Electronic journals/magazines	Library books
Print Indexes	Electronic/Web-based indexes	Reference Desk/Library Staff
Web/Internet	Print journals/magazines	Other _____

4. What were the most useful library resources for your research? Why?

5. Have you attended library instruction sessions, taught by a Librarian, for other courses?

    _____ Yes   _____ No
    If yes, how many? _____

6. Do you think a presentation on library resources for this class would have been helpful?

    _____Yes   Comments:

    _____No

7. What would you like to know about library research?

Use back of sheet for additional comments
Thanks!

174 - Documents: *Feedback With/Without Instruction*

DOCUMENTS :
Assessment of Faculty Information Literacy

Faculty Information Literacy Instrument and Attitude Survey

Please complete the following questions to the best of your knowledge.
Your comments will be anonymous.
Do not be offended if some of the questions seem too easy. This data will be
compared to that gathered from students taking a similar instrument.

Special Note: In Questions 1-21 the terms "research paper" and "term paper" refer to
lower-level undergraduate research, not specialized or graduate research.

1. Circle the most accurate statement:
   a. All information is available on the Internet.
   b. The Internet contains a mix of information of varying quality.
   c. The Internet contains mainly popular information sources.
   d. The Internet contains nothing of value.

2. Which of the following would not be considered a primary source?
   a. a speech
   b. an autobiography
   c. a textbook
   d. a television interview

3. The service offered in most public and academic libraries that allows you to get almost
   any publication you need is called:
   a. reserves
   b. reference
   c. interlibrary loan
   d. full-text

4. Items in great demand (often placed on faculty reading lists) that are available for limited
   loan periods in a special section of the library are:
   a. microfilm material
   b. newspaper material
   c. reference material
   d. reserve material

5. A place in a library staffed by someone who answers questions and provides help in using
   the library, conducting research, and locating information is:
   a. a reference desk
   b. a periodicals room
   c. a computer lab

6. A short paragraph that describes the scope, focus, and value of an item is:
   a. an article
   b. a citation
   c. an annotation
   d. a footnote

7. Books kept in a college library are now normally located through:
   a. the card catalog
   b. periodical indexes
   c. a printed list updated each month
   d. the online library catalog

8. It is often advisable to begin research for a term paper in what section of the library?
   a. circulating books
   b. journals and periodicals
   c. reserve collection
   d. reference collection

9. When selecting materials for research papers from the Internet, which criterion is least important?
   a. currency
   b. authority
   c. frequency
   d. objectivity
   e. accuracy

10. Anything you find on the Internet is yours for the taking.
    a. true
    b. false

11. When performing a search with an Internet search engine or online database, which will bring up the most items?
    a. gun OR control
    b. gun AND control
    c. gun NOT control

12. When evaluating web pages for possible use in research papers, students should be most cautious of those from which domain?
    a. .org
    b. .com
    c. .gov
    d. .edu

13. Which of these is not a type of Internet search tool?
    a. browser (e.g., Microsoft Internet Explorer)
    b. meta search engine (e.g., Dogpile)
    c. search engine (e.g., Altavista)
    d. subject directory (e.g., Yahoo)

14. Which of the following Internet search structures is correct when looking for web sites on drunk driving in New Mexico?
    a. "drunk driving"+ "New Mexico"+
    b. +"drunk driving" +"New Mexico"
    c. + drunk driving + New Mexico
    d. "+drunk driving +New Mexico"

15. Which would you normally not find listed in a library catalog?
    a. a video
    b. a book
    c. an article
    d. a government document

16. Which of the following citations describes a journal article?
    a. Doctor Zhivago. New York: MGM/UA Home Video, c1988.
    b. Mitchell, T. R. (1987). People in organizations: An introduction to organizational behavior (3rd ed.). New York: McGraw-Hill.
    c. Coltheart, M., & Curtis, B. (1993). Models of reading aloud. Psychological Review, 100(2), 589-599.
    d. American Library Association, Presidential Committee on Information Literacy. (1989). Final report. Retrieved on April 15, 2000 from the World Wide Web: http://www.ala.org/acrl/nili/ilit1st.html.

17. Articles from which one of the following periodicals are consistently appropriate for use a research paper?
    a. Science
    b. Redbook
    c. Atlantic Monthly
    d. Newsweek
    e. Psychology Today

18. Research papers should not ordinarily include articles from which of these sources?
    a. newspapers
    b. scholarly journals
    c. peer-reviewed journals
    d. popular magazines

19. The term to describe a list of books, articles, web pages and other materials that have some relationship to each other is:
    a. an autobiography
    b. a bibliography
    c. a biography
    d. a footnote

20. A summary of the contents of an article, book, web page, or other item is:
    a. an abstract
    b. an index
    c a pamphlet
    d. a periodical

21. Which of the following is not an appropriate step in writing a research paper?
    a. evaluating each resource obtained for relevance to the topic
    b. narrowing the topic
    c. basing the paper on the first sources that came up when searching the topic in the library databases
    d. revising the first draft for grammatical, formatting, and organizational problems

Background and Personal Information

22. At what type of institution do you teach?

23. What is your gender?
    a. male
    b. female

24. What is your teaching category?
    a. full-time
    b. adjunct

25. How many years have you been teaching?

26. What types of courses do you teach?
    a. humanities
    b. social sciences
    c. mathematics or sciences
    d. vocational or technical
    e. other

27. How frequently do you schedule a library instruction session with library staff?
    a. never
    b. occasionally
    c. usually
    d. always

28. To what extent do you integrate library research requirements into your curriculum?
    a. never
    b. rarely
    c. sometimes
    d. frequently
    e. always

29. How would you rate the overall information literacy level of your students? Information literacy is defined as the ability to locate, understand, interpret, evaluate, and communicate appropriate information for any need from appropriate sources.
    a. low
    b. medium
    c. high

30. Have you received formal library research instruction in the past five years?
    a. yes
    b. no

31. Have you had any formal instruction on researching on the Internet?
    a. yes
    b. no

32. How often have you visited a library within the past year?
    a. never
    b. rarely
    c. sometimes
    d. frequently
    e. daily

33. To what extent do you enjoy reading for pleasure?
    a. not at all
    b. a little
    c. some
    d. moderately
    e. extremely

34. Do you have access to the Internet in the following locales? (Choose all that apply.)
    a. work
    b. home
    c. friend or relative's home
    d. public library
    e. school

35. What is your comfort level with computers?
    1. terrified
    2. can fumble around
    3. competent
    4. expert

36. What is your comfort level with the college library?
    1. terrified
    2. can fumble around
    3. competent
    4. expert

37. Before you become frustrated, how often can you find what you need on the Internet?
    1. never
    2. rarely
    3. sometimes
    4. frequently

38. How would you assess your overall knowledge of how to conduct library research?
    1. poor
    2. fair
    3. good
    4. excellent

39. Should college students receive information literacy instruction?
    a. If yes, how should this instruction be provided?

    b. If no, please explain

40. Should faculty be offered information literacy instruction?
    a. If yes, how should this instruction be provided?

    b. If no, please explain

41. Please list the steps you would take to find information on body piercing.

1._____

2._____

3. _____

4. _____

5. _____

6. _____

7. _____

8. _____

9. _____

10._____

http://personal.lig.bellsouth.net/lig/a/n/annemoor/facili.html
Page last updated on Sunday, January 28, 2001
Contact person: Anne Moore (annem@library.umass.edu)

DOCUMENTS :
Cross-Campus Assessment of Information Literacy

Assessment of Information Literacy Skills At The College of Saint Rose

Results

100 undergraduate volunteers (Freshmen, Sophomores, Juniors and Seniors) took an 18-item assessment of their information literacy skills.   Incentive: $5.00 upon completion.

This is the form used for the research. Comments that did not appear on the assessment form show here in italic boldface. There was a Form A and a Form B, with questions in different order, and minor differences in the information sought (e.g. finding the call numbers for different books). Data has been combined here into one form. [Steve Black]

INSTRUCTIONS

Answer every question to the best of your ability.

On Part 1, guess if you do not know the answer for sure.

On Part 2, if you cannot find the answer, write down "could not find answer in X minutes," where the X is your estimate of how long you tried.

When you have completed this, take it to the reference desk to receive your $5.

This project was funded by the Janice Graham Newkirk Award.

I am a

29 Freshman *(Average score 10.81 out of 18, or 60.06%)*

15 Sophomore *(Average score 11.17 out of 18, or 62.06%)*

29 Junior *(Average score 11.03 out of 18, or 61.28%)*

27 Senior *(Average score 11.44 out of 18, or 63.56%)*

 Note: The research plan called for 25 from each class. An extra effort was made towards the end to recruit more sophomores, but we ran short. The assessment was reopened to all students at the end of the Fall 2000 semester. It is an intriguing mystery why sophomores were under represented.

I have attended classes conducted by a librarian

35 Never *(Average score 10.53)*

37 Once *(Average score 11.18)*

24 2 or 3 times *(Average score 11.54)*

4   4 or more times *(Average score 10.17)*

I have asked for help from a librarian at the reference desk

17 Never *(Average score 10.63)*

11 Once *(Average score 10.05)*

34 2 or 3 times *(Average score 11.00)*

38 4 or more times *(Average score 11.25)*

I would personally rate my ability to find and use information as

6   Excellent *(Average score 11.92)*

51 Good *(Average score 11.25)*

39 Fair *(Average score 10.71)*

4   Poor *(Average score 9.75)*

Part 1. Answer the multiple choice questions in Part 1 using only what you know, without looking anything up or asking anyone for help. Put a check in the box of the correct answer.

ANSWER ALL QUESTIONS

Number of answers (n=100) shown to left as a percentage. Correct answers appear in bold. Some percentages do not total 100 because of blank responses.

1. Which of the following has records showing the locations of all the books and journals owned by this library?

> 36% **Online catalog**
> 6% EBSCOhost
> 3% FirstSearch
> 55% All of the above

2. What would be the best resource to use to find a citation to a magazine article published in 1940 about Franklin Roosevelt?

> 45% EBSCOhost Academic Search Elite
> 3% WorldCat
> 46% **Reader's Guide to Periodical Literature**
> 5% Online catalog

3. Which of these would be a citation to a book?

> 70% **Smith, R. (1999). *Bones*. New York: Big Press.**
> 26% Smith, R. (1999). Bones. *Paleoanthropology*, 10, 34-66.
> 2% Smith, R. (1999). Available online at http://www.bones.org.
> 1% Smith, R. (1999). *Bones*. Unpublished manuscript.

4. Who created the Neil Hellman Library home page at http://www.strose.edu/Library/li_hp.htm?

> 5% The staff at EBSCOhost
> 89% **Librarians at The College of Saint Rose**
> 4% Librarians at the New York State Library
> 1% The staff at Yahoo

5. Interlibrary loan (ILL) is a system for Saint Rose students to

> 0% Purchase books and journals
> 1% Borrow books owned by the Neil Hellman Library
> 87% **Get books and articles that are not owned by the Neil Hellman Library**
> 11% Travel to area libraries, and check books out of them

6. Which of the following would be the best for identifying any book NOT owned by the Neil Hellman Library?

> 54% EBSCOhost Academic Search
> 11% Modern Language Association (MLA) International Bibliography
> 8% Neil Hellman Library Periodicals List
> 26% **WorldCat**

7. The sole, exclusive right to profit from a creative work (e.g. a novel) is called

   4% Plagiarism
   93% **Copyright**
   3% Trademark
   0% Fair use

8. Which of the following search statements would be BEST to find an article about the life of dolphins in the Florida Keys?

   11% Dolphins AND ocean
   51% **Dolphins AND Florida NOT football**
   1% Keys AND marine life
   37% Florida Keys OR Dolphins

9. Which of the following is the BEST way to check the accuracy of a web page?

   11% e-mail the author of the web page
   0% ask a friend
   2% assume that the information is incorrect
   87% **check the information against information from other sources**

Part 2: Use library resources to find the answers to each of the following. Everything you need can be found somewhere on the first floor of the library.

Correct answer is below question number of correct responses is in bold italics. The answers were graded fairly leniently, and half credit was given for partially correct answers.

10. What is the call number for the book *The Search for Life in the Universe*?

   574.999 G624S
   92 correct

11. Write the citation for an article about George Patton that was published in a magazine in 1943:

   Varies, could be one of several from Reader's Guide to Periodical Literature from that time.
   8.5 correct

   (This is the lowest number correct of any question. Many students wrote in something indicating that they searched online to find the answer.

12. Write the citation for this bibliographic record in APA style, as it would appear in the Works Cited, OR write it in MLA style as it would appear in the References. *(Printed assessment included an image of an index citation).*

   Graded correct if the elements were all there in the right order. Punctuation not graded.
   68 correct

13. Use the library's home page to answer: What is the e-mail address to ask a librarian a question?

refdesk@rosnet.strose.edu

88.5 correct

(half right if they wrote contact for web page creator, who is also a reference librarian)

14. What is the web address for placing interlibrary loan (ILL) requests online?

http://www.strose.edu/Library/ill/webzap.htm

82.5 correct

15. Use WorldCat to find an item about kookaburras. Write down the author, the title, and publication date of the item.

Can be one of several citations, but must be to a WorldCat item (not to a journal article).

49 correct

16. If you got the copyright today on something you created, how long would the copyright be in effect?

Life of the author plus 70 years.

9.5 correct

This question was really about whether a student would know to use a ready reference source (e.g. dictionary, encyclopedia) to find the information. Life + 50 years was accepted as correct, since that is the information given in older reference sources.

17. Print or write out the citation for a journal article published within the last 3 years on the topic: power, money, and business ethics. (If you print it out, turn in the printout together with these pages).

Citation must be the result of the search "power AND money AND business ethics".

Half credit for something that uses the words but is not on the topic.

52.5 correct

18. Take a look at http://www.asha.org. List 3 reasons why this web site is or is not a high quality information resource.

Answer should be based on the criteria of authority, accuracy, objectivity, currency, and coverage.

76.5 correct

This was very difficult to grade. Any reasonable standards were given partial credit. A strict grading on the 5 criteria would have yielded a much lower number correct.

Neil Hellman Library
The College of Saint Rose
392 Western Ave.
Albany, NY 12203

[Developer/Contact: Steve Black blacks@mail.strose.edu]